Football Math

TOUCHDOWN ACTIVITIES AND PROJECTS
FOR GRADES 4-8

Jack Coffland and David A. Coffland

GoodYearBooks

An Imprint of ScottForesman
A Division of HarperCollinsPublishers

GoodYearBooks are available for most basic
curriculum subjects plus many enrichment
areas. For more GoodYearBooks, contact your
local bookseller or educational dealer. For a
complete catalog with information about other
GoodYearBooks, please write:

GoodYearBooks
ScottForesman
1900 East Lake Avenue
Glenview, IL 60025

Illustrations by Douglas Klauba.
Design by Patricia Lenihan-Barbee.

0-673-36174-8

4 5 6 7 8 9–EQ– 02 01 00 99 98 97 96

Introduction for parents and teachers

When giving students in grades 4 through 8 problems to solve, we must be certain that they have practiced a wide variety of problems. By the time students are finished with the eighth grade, they should be proficient with problem-solving involving:

- Whole Number Computation
- Fraction Computation
- Decimal Computation
- Percent Computation

One problem classification system used by many mathematicians includes both. In other words, it is no longer appropriate to give students problems that simply review computational operations that have just been taught.

Routine problems

"Routine problems" are defined as those problems that ask students to apply a mathematical process they have learned in class in a real-life, problem-solving situation. This book defines two types of routine problems:

1. Algorithmic problems:
These are word problems (story problems) that ask children to read the problem, figure out the computational procedure required, and then apply that computational algorithm to solve the problem. For example:
Bobby scored 6 touchdowns in last night's game. Each touchdown is worth 6 points. How many points did he score in all?

2. Multi-step problems:
These are algorithmic problems that

demand two or more computational steps in order to obtain the answer. For example:
Last year the Bruisers won three-quarters of their 12 games. This year they won 5 games. How many wins did they have over the two seasons?
Similar problems can be made with decimals or percents.

Non-routine problems

In recent years math educators have focused additional energy on "non-routine" problems—those that challenge the learner in some way. The different kinds of "non-routine" problems in this book are:

1. Challenge problems:
Problems of this type are non-routine in that the child does not know how to solve them from memory. They require the use of heuristics, the act of inventing steps. It is the true test of problem-solving ability. Examples are:

A one-kilometer train enters a one-kilometer tunnel moving at 30 kilometers per hour. How much time will pass from the time the engine enters the tunnel until the caboose comes out of the tunnel?

Problems of this type are the final challenge in math. We cannot quit until

we have challenged children to invent or create solutions to problems. The professional scientist, engineer, or mathematician all work to create ideas, not to simply rehash old ideas. But the myth of mathematics learning has always been that only people in these professions must solve problems. The truth of the situation is that every day the carpenter, the clerical worker, or the grocery store clerk also invent solutions to problems.

2. Mini-project pproblems:
These problems are "process" problems, not simple story problems. They are often open-ended in that different students may obtain different answers. The process is more important than the product; the process stresses such things as multiple steps, differences in answers, and discussion of considerations to see if everyone agrees. For example:

How much money do we need to take with us on the field trip to the stadium?

Notice that this situation depends upon several different variables; not everyone will take the same amount of money on the trip. Solving mini-project problems teaches children that not all problems have simple answers, nor do they all have one answer.

Long-term projects
Finally, since this book is meant to capture the interest of students by combining mathematics and football, we have suggested project problems. These are not really math problems; they are projects that the student can undertake that require the use of math and a knowledge of football. They are meant to be fun and to make math and football the child's hobbies.

Resources

The Official National Football League 1993 Record and Fact Book. *New York: National Football League/Workman, 1993.*

Meserole, Mike, ed. 1993 Information Please Sports Almanac. *Boston: Houghton-Mifflin, 1993.*

1993 and 1994 High School Football Handbook. Kansas City, MO: *The National Federation of State High School Associations, 1994.*

The 1993 High School Football Casebook. Kansas City, MO: *The National Federation of State High School Associations, 1993.*

The 1993 High School Football Rules. Kansas City, MO: *The National Federation of State High School Associations, 1993.*

The Sports Illustrated 1993 Sports Almanac and Record Book. *New York: Time, 1993.*

Introduction for students

This book is about football; it contains a great deal of interesting material about football—professional football, college football, and even high school football. But it is also about math. It asks you to solve math problems that stem from football statistics, stories, and situations.

This material attempts to explain some interesting things about football. For example, you can see how a college passing rating is determined. You will be given a problem to figure out one example yourself, but you will enjoy the book much more if you tackle the project on rating college passers. Collect statistics on your favorite quarterback; then see if you can figure out his rating before you read it in the paper. Or, if you are playing football, keep track of your own statistics and rate yourself!

The book also contains a number of facts about college and professional football. For example, who holds the career rushing record for the Dallas Cowboys? What college team had the best record during the last ten years? The information is presented in math problems—have fun solving them or give them to your friends to solve. You will already know the answers. Enjoy!

Contents

Projects

ACTIVITIES

Miami Dolphin records

Solve the following problems.

1. Good tickets on the 50-yard line to a Miami Dolphins football game cost $26 each. If you wish to buy four of them for your family, how much will you have to spend?

2. In 1984 Dan Marino set the NFL record for throwing 48 touchdown passes in one season. Since each touchdown is worth six points, how many points did the Dolphins score on Marino passes that year?

3. Dan Marino's favorite targets for many years were Mark Clayton and Mark Duper, known as the "Marks Brothers." Clayton caught 550 of Marino's passes, while Duper caught 480. How many passes did they catch all together?

4. In 1992 the Dolphins gained 1,525 yards rushing and 3,975 yards passing. A team's total offense is calculated by combining the rushing and passing yards. What was the Dolphins' "Total Offense" figure for 1992?

5. The San Francisco 49ers led the league in total offense with 6,369 gained yards in 1992. How many more yards did the 49ers gain than the Dolphins?

6. Mercury Morris rushed for more yards in one game than any other Dolphin running back. His record is 197 rushing yards gained in a single game. How many yards would he gain in a season if he had rushed for that many yards in every game? (Fact: Each team now plays 16 games in the regular season.)

Lincoln's big win

Solve the following problems.

1. The Lincoln Junior High football team scored a big win over Central Junior High. The quarterback passed for 325 yards, and the running backs ran for 279 yards. How many total yards did Lincoln gain on its way to its easy victory?

2. Lincoln's star wide receiver caught eight passes for a total of 256 yards. What was his average gain for each of the eight receptions?

3. Central Junior High did not have a very good day. They only gained 136 yards total, and 48 of these came on one good pass play. How many yards did Central gain on all the rest of their plays?

4. After a winning game, the Lincoln cheerleaders do a pushup for each point the team scored. Lincoln has 12 cheerleaders. If they each did 35 pushups, how many pushups did they have to do at the end of the game?

5. Lincoln let every person on its team play in an effort to keep from running up the score. If they have 37 offensive players and 39 defensive players, how many players did Lincoln play in the game?

6. The game was played on a very hot day. Each of Lincoln's players drank five glasses of water during the game. How many cups of water did the trainers have to fill during the game? (*Hint:* Where can you find the total number of football players on Lincoln's team?)

Debbie's dogs

Debbie and her club have decided to run the concession stand at the high school football game as a way to raise money for the club. She wants to figure how much food she should buy and how much they sell for each game. You can help her.

1. Debbie knows that the high school football field will seat 3,000 people. The principal has been able to predict that, based on past years, half of those people will buy a hot dog. How many hot dogs should Debbie buy if she expects a sell-out crowd?

_____

2. Debbie also knows that about two-fifths of a crowd will buy coffee. How many cups should she buy if the athletic department expects to have a sell-out?

_____

3. For the first game, the crowd is small. Only 1,434 people attend the first game. If two-thirds of them bought a cold drink (it was a hot night), how many soft drinks did Debbie and her club sell?

_____

4. During the second game Debbie decided to try selling a new snack—nachos. The attendance at the game was 2,464 people, and Debbie sold nachos to three-quarters of them. How many orders of nachos did Debbie sell?

_____

5. For the game played on Halloween night, Debbie and her crew dressed in their best costumes and served hot cider. The crowd was small because most people stayed home to meet the "trick or treaters." Only 1,566 people came to the game, but five-sixths of them had the hot cider. How many cups of hot cider did Debbie sell that night?

_____

6. During the last game it was really cold, but 2,985 people attended the game anyway. Debbie counted the coffee cups that were used and figured that four-fifths of the people bought a cup of coffee. How many cups of coffee did Debbie and her club sell that night?

_____

Debbie's dollars and sense

The club members worked so hard selling things that they wanted to know how much money they made. You can help Debbie figure the profits from last night's game.

1. Soft drinks make more money for the club than anything else they sell. Soft drinks come in only one size; it sells for a $1.00. From that dollar, 82¢ is profit. After counting cups, Debbie knows that she sold 934 soft drinks. How much money did the club make on soft drink sales?

_____

2. Hot dogs sell for $1.50. Debbie and her club make 78¢ on each hot dog sale. If they sold 576 hot dogs last night, how much money did they make on hot dog sales?

_____

3. Candy bars are not a good money maker. They cost $1.00, but only 36¢ of that is profit. If they sold 164 candy bars last night, how much did they make selling candy bars?

_____

4. A cup of coffee sells for only 75¢, but 55¢ of that is profit. How much did Debbie and her hard-working crew make selling coffee last night if they sold 634 cups of coffee?

_____

5. Nachos sell for $2.00, and $1.05 of that is profit. Debbie sold 1,246 containers of nachos and cheese last night. How much profit did the club earn on those sales?

_____

6. Figure the total profit Debbie and her club made last night on the items listed in problems 1 through 5.

_____

Challenge problem

Do you think that taking over the concession stand was a good way for Debbie's club to make money? You may need to know that they worked 6 home games, and they made about the same amount of money for the other nights as they did on this night.

Quarterback stats

League statistics for the Frontier League were released yesterday. They indicate the percentage completion figures for all of the quarterbacks in the league. Only part of the statistics are shown below; work with the numbers to complete the figures. Remember that all percentage completion figures are rounded off, so you will have to round off all of your answers to the nearest whole number. *(After all, you can't complete half of a pass.)*

Frontier League quarterback statistics

Quarterback and team	Passes attempted	Percentage completed	Passes completed
Tom Davis, Bengals	148	52%	——
Mike Irving, Broncos	91	——	38
Jimmy Anderson, Vandals	——	47%	58
Dan Buratto, Bantams	156	——	72
Steve Johnson, Grayhounds	——	41%	43
Bob Myers, Bulldogs	112	45%	——

1. The table shows that Tom Davis threw 148 passes. He completed 52% of them. How many passes to his receivers did he complete?

2. What percentage of his passes did Mike Irving complete?

3. How many passes did Jimmy Anderson attempt?

4. Dan Buratto completed what percentage of his passes?

5. How many passes did Steve Johnson attempt?

6. How many passes did Bob Myers complete?

7. From these statistics, who do you think should be the all-star quarterback? Why?

Deeee-fense

Make the following computations about the Frontier League defensive players and answer the questions that follow.

Frontier League defensive statistics

Defensive player and position	Total sacks	Tackles made	Fumbles recovered	Passes intercepted
Larry Minor, LB	2	42	6	1
Jon Davidson, DL	14	23	1	0
Stan Smith, LB	12	67	4	1
Jon Echohawk, CB	1	24	2	9
Howard Gardner, DL	6	28	1	0
Claude Gibbons, CB	0	56	2	3

Position code: LB = Linebacker, DL = Defensive lineman, CB = Corner back

1. Larry Minor recovered 40% of the fumbles that his team recovered. How many fumbles did his team recover all together?

_____

If Larry's team played six games this season, would you say the coach is happy with the number of fumbles his defensive team recovered? Why or why not?

_____

_____

_____

2. When you total all of his defensive statistics, you find that Stan Smith was responsible for ending 84 plays. If the defense was on the field for 276 plays in their six games, what percentage of the plays did Stan end personally?

_____

Do you think Stan is the star of his defensive team? Why?

_____

3. Jon Echohawk intercepted nine passes; only 30 passes were thrown in his direction. What percentage of the passes thrown to players on his side of the field did Jon intercept?

_____

If you were the coach of a team that had to play Jon, would you throw many passes to his side of the field? Why or why not?

_____

4. Claude Gibbons made 40% of all the tackles made by his team. How many tackles did his team make all together?

_____

Do you think Claude plays on a team with a winning record? Why or why not?

_____

_____

Beasts of the east

The National Football Conference Eastern Division is known as a tough league where the teams like to play "slam-bang" football. The teams are known as having tough defenses and offenses that like to run the ball right down each other's throats. Let's examine those stereotypes.

National Football Conference – Eastern division team record for a single season		
Team	Rushing record	Passing record
Cardinals	1605	4614
Cowboys	1713	3980
Eagles	1512	3808
Giants	1516	4044
Redskins	1347	4109

1. Look at the individual season rushing record. Find the average number of rushing yards for these five teams. (Carry out your answer to the nearest tenth.) _____

2. Now look at the single season passing records for each of the teams. Find the average number of passing yards for these five teams. (Do you need a decimal in this answer?) _____

3. Now use your averages to answer this question: How much larger is the average passing record over the average running record for these teams? (Carry your answer out to one decimal point.) _____

4. Let's look at how these season records translate into game statistics. Consider the records for the Dallas Cowboys. Emmitt Smith holds the season rushing record for Dallas. If Dallas played 16 games in the regular season, and if Emmitt played in all 16 games, what was his average rushing total for each game? (Round your answer to the nearest hundredth.) _____

5. The Cardinals had the worst record in the NFC-Eastern Division over the last several years, but Neil Lomax, the quarterback who holds their single-season yardage record for passing, has the highest record of all the teams. If Neil played in all 16 of the Cardinal games, what was his average number of passing yards for each game? (Again, round your answer to the nearest hundredth.) _____

Bobcats victory

It was a wild ball game at the high school last night. The score was Bobcats 48, Grizzlies 42. Let's look at some of the statistics to see why the score was so high.

1. Bobby Nelson, a Bobcats wide receiver, caught 12 passes. He averaged 14.72 yards per catch. How many total yards did he gain on his pass receptions?

2. Timmy Johnson, the Grizzlies quarterback, completed 34 passes for 387 yards. What was his average gain per completion? (Figure your answer to the nearest hundredth.)

3. Big Jon Crump, the Bobcats fullback, ran for 137 yards on 16 carries. What was his average gain per carry? (Round off your answer out to the nearest tenth.)

4. There were only three punts in the game. The Grizzlies punted all three times for 121 yards. What was the punter's average distance per kick? (Round off your answer to the nearest tenth.)

5. The Grizzlies had a hard time running the ball. Three Grizzly running backs gained only 48.7 yards, 23.2 yards, and 17.5 yards respectively. How many total yards did the Grizzlies gain rushing the ball?

Challenge problem

When a score is this high, do you think the offensive team improved their statistics? Do you think a defensive team improved their statistics? Why or why not?

Why is it called football?

NFL defenses are so strong that a team wants to score every time they are in the "red zone." It is also important that a team comes away with at least a field goal if the offense drives inside the opponent's 40-yard line. For that reason field goal kickers are extremely important offensive weapons. Look at the following statistics for four of the better kickers in the National Football Conference.

Field goal statistics

Four National Football Conference kickers

Kicker	PATs	F goals	Total points
Morton Anderson	33/34	29/34	120
Lin Elliott	47/48	24/35	119
Faud Raveiz	45/45	19/25	102
Jason Hanson	30/30	__/26	93

Answer the following questions about these statistics:

1. How many total points did all four kickers score?

_____

2. If Morton Anderson made 29 field goals, and if each field goal is worth three points, how many points did he score on field goals?

_____

3. How many field goals did Jason Hanson make if he scored 63 of his points on field goals?

_____

4. How many more points did Lin Elliott score than Faud Raveiz?

_____

5. What was the total number of extra points kicked by all of the kickers listed?

_____

Challenge problem

After examining the statistics listed above, fill in the missing items for Pittsburgh Steelers kicker Gary Anderson:

Name	PATs	F goals	Total points
Gary Anderson	__/31	28/36	113

They get a kick out of this

Use the table below to solve the following problems.

American Football Conference

Kicker statistics

Kicker	PATs	FGoals	Total points
Pete Stoyanovich	34/36	—/37	124
Steve Christie	43/44	24/30	115
Nick Lowery	39/39	22/24	105
Al Del Greco	41/41	21/—	104

1. Pete Stoyanovich attempted 37 field goals. He made 81% of his attempts. Fill in the blank on the chart that tells how many field goals he made.

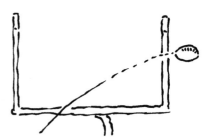

2. These four kickers missed only three points after touchdowns (PATs). What was the percentage of kicks made for the total of all the kicks attempted by these four kickers?

3. Al Del Greco made 21 field goals; he made 77.7% of the kicks he attempted. Fill in the blank that tells how many field goals he attempted during the 1992-93 season.

4. Now that you have completed the chart, find the percentage of field goals that were made for all of the field goals attempted by these four kickers.

5. A kicker really helps his team when he makes a 50-yard or longer field goal, because his team then scores points when they did not get close to the goal line. Pete Stoyanovich attempted eight kicks from beyond 50 yards. He made three. What percentage did he make?

AFC rushing leaders

For a running back in the National Football League, the goal is to rush for 1,000 yards in a season. Five players in the American Conference accomplished that goal during the 1992 season:

1992 thousand-yard rushers

American Football Conference

Player	Att	Yards	Avg.	Long	TD
Barry Foster, Pitt	390	1690	4.3	69	11
Thurman Thomas, Buf	312	1487	4.8	44	9
Lorenzo White, Hou	265	1226	4.6	44	7
Harold Green, Cin	265	1170	4.4	53	2
Chris Warren, Sea	223	1017	4.6	52	3

1. How many more yards did Barry Foster gain than Harold Green?

2. Barry Foster and Thurman Thomas have been the most famous rushing backs in the American Conference for several years. How many yards did the two of them gain all together? What is the total number of times they carried the ball?

3. How much further was Barry Foster's longest run from scrimmage than that of Chris Warren?

_____

4. Barry Foster had the most carries; Chris Warren had the least number of plays where he carried the ball. Compare the two amounts. How many more times did Foster carry the ball than Warren?

_____

5. Thurman Thomas scored nine rushing touchdowns. How many points did he score with those touchdowns? *(He also scored three touchdowns with pass receptions. How many points did he score from both rushing and passing touchdowns?)*

_____

_____

6. Thurman Thomas has been an outstanding running back for several years. Imagine that he played for eight seasons, and he gained exactly the same number of yards in each season as he did in 1992. If this was true, how many total rushing yards would he have for his career?

_____

NFC rushing leaders

For a running back in the National Football League, the goal is to rush for 1,000 yards in a season. Eight players in the National Conference accomplished that goal during the 1992 season:

1992 Thousand-yard rushers

National Football Conference

Player	Att	Yards	Avg.	Long	TD
Emmitt Smith, Dal	373	1713	4.6	68	18
Barry Sanders, Det	312	1352	4.3	55	9
Terry Allen, Min	266	1201	4.5	51	13
Reggie Cobb, TBay	310	1171	3.8	25	9
Rodney Hampton, Gia	257	1141	4.4	63	14
Cleveland Gary, Rams	279	1125	4.0	63	7
Herschel Walker, Phil	267	1070	4.0	38	8
Ricky Watters, SF	206	1013	4.9	43	9

1. How many yards did Emmitt Smith and Barry Sanders gain all together?

2. Smith scored 18 touchdowns. How many points did he make?

3. Emmitt Smith carried the ball the most number of times, and Ricky Watters carried it the least number of times. How many more carries did Emmitt Smith have than Ricky Watters?

4. Emmitt Smith has the longest run from scrimmage for any of these rushing backs; Reggie Cobb had the shortest "longest run." How much longer was Emmitt Smith's longest run than Cobb's?

5. Herschel Walker has played professional football longer than any of the other players. If he played for 12 seasons, and gained exactly 1,070 yards for each of those seasons, what would his career rushing statistic be?

What does the "average run" statistic tell you? Discuss what happens each time Ricky Watters carries the ball. Compare that to what happens each time Reggie Cobb carries the ball.

Home field advantage

Much is made of the "home field advantage" in sports. Is it easier to win at home? In football the answer appears to be "yes." All but three AFC teams have a winning record at home for the last ten years; only two AFC teams have a winning record on the road over the last ten years. But some teams enjoy even a larger advantage. Use the table on page 18 to answer the questions below.

1. Denver plays its games in Mile High Stadium. It is hard for teams to perform well at high altitudes if they are not used to them. Denver has the highest home-field winning advantage of any team in the NFL. What is Denver's winning percentage?

2. Miami also has a "home field advantage." Games are usually played during the afternoon hours, which can be especially hot and humid in Miami. As the game goes on, teams often seem to "wilt" in that intense heat. Using the information given in the table, find how many games Miami won at home in the last ten years. How many did they lose? (Remember to round your answers to whole numbers; you can't lose half a game!)

Top home field records

AFC teams—1983–92

Team	Games	Wins	Losses	Ties	Percentages
Denver	80	63	17	0	
Miami	79			0	.709
Kansas City	79	52	27	0	
L.A. Raiders		51		0	.638
Pittsburgh	70	49	30	0	

3. Compute the losing percentage for Kansas City. What percentage of its home games did Kansas City lose? What percentage did they win? *(Note that all percentage figures in the table are rounded to the nearest thousandth; round yours off to that position also.)*

4. Given the winning percentage for the Los Angeles Raiders, how many games did they play at home in the years between 1983 and 1992? Can you tell how many games they lost at home in those ten years?

5. Calculate the home-field winning percentage for the Pittsburgh Steelers.

More home cooking

The NFC leaders in home-field advantage in the years between 1983 and 1992 are shown in the table. No percentage figures are shown.

Top home field records

AFC Teams—1983–92

Team	Games	Wins	Losses	Ties	Percentages
Washington	79	60	19	0	
Chicago	80	60	20	0	
San Francisco	79	58	21	0	
N.Y. Giants	80	54	26	0	
New Orleans	79	48	31	0	
Minnesota	80	47	33	0	

1. Calculate the winning percentage for each team listed in the chart. Enter your answers into the chart.

2. In the NFC, San Francisco was the only team to have a higher winning percentage on the road that it did at home *(for the seasons from 1983-1992)*. Its record on the road for those ten years was:

Wins 62   Losses 17   Ties 1

Calculate its winning percentage for the road. *(Note: The tie must be used to obtain the total games played.)*

Challenge problem

What was San Francisco's winning percentage on the road? How much higher was that than their winning percentage at home? Why do you think they were the only team in those ten years to win more on the road than they did at home? *(A point to consider: The road winning percentage for most teams is not even close to their home-field winning percentage.)*

"Shoes" and "Poppa Bear"

At the end of the 1993 NFL season, there were five NFL coaches who had won more than 200 total games in their careers. They were:

NFL coaches won/lost record

Through the 1993 season

Coach	Won	Lost	Tied
Don Shula	327	158	6
George Halas	324	151	31
Tom Landry	270	178	6
Curly Lambeau	229	134	22
Chuck Noll	209	156	1

1. During the 1993 season Don "Shoes" Shula passed George "Poppa Bear" Halas in the "games won" category. Shula had won more games than any other NFL coach in history. Until just a few years ago, Shula and Tom Landry ran "neck and neck" in the race to see who would surpass Halas first. However, Landry was let go as coach of the Dallas Cowboys, so he ceased to add to his "wins" column. As of 1993, how many more games had Shula won than Landry?

2. As of 1993, Don Shula was the only active coach on the list of coaches with over 200 wins. Chuck Knox was second on the list of active coaches; he had won 184 games. How many games did Shula and Knox win together?

_____

3. Very few coaches stay with the same team for their entire career. For example, Don Shula coached for both the Baltimore _(now Indianapolis)_ Colts and the Miami Dolphins. But George Halas, Tom Landry, and Chuck Noll accomplished all of their victories with one team. Halas only coached the Chicago Bears; Landry only coached the Dallas Cowboys; and Noll only coached the Pittsburg Steelers. How many games did these three coaches win all together?

_____

4. Curly Lambeau coached the Green Bay Packers, the Washington Redskins, and the old Chicago Cardinals. He was a head coach in the NFL for 33 years. On the average, how many games did he win each year? _(Since you can't win part of a game, don't worry about your remainder when you finish doing the problem!)_

_____

Challenge problem

Why does Halas have so many more tie games than Shula?

_____

"Shoes" and "Poppa Bear"

The "best of the best"

At the end of the 1992 NFL season, there were five NFL coaches who had won more than 200 total games in their careers. They were:

NFL coaches won/lost record				
Through the 1993 season				
Coach	*Won*	*Lost*	*Tied*	*Years*
Don Shula	*327*	*158*	*6*	*40*
George Halas	*324*	*151*	*31*	*30*
Tom Landry	*270*	*178*	*6*	*39*
Curly Lambeau	*229*	*134*	*22*	*33*
Chuck Noll	*209*	*156*	*1*	*23*

1. Figure the average record for each coach, given the number of years that each coached in the NFL through 1992. Compute the average number of wins, losses, and ties for each individual.

2. Compare records. From the averages, who won the greatest number of games each season? Who lost the greatest number of games each season?

Challenge problem

Is it fair to compare the number of victories in a season over the last fifty years? Why or why not? Would it be better to compute winning percentages? Can you compute the winning percentage for each coach? (*Note: Do not count tie games in any manner while creating your computational situation.*)

Monsters of the Midway

Solve the following problems.

1. Walter Payton holds the all-time season rushing mark for the Chicago Bears. He rushed for 1,842 yards in 1977. In those days teams only played 14 games in a season. What was the average number of yards that Payton gained each game?

2. Walter Payton holds both the Chicago Bear record and the National Football League record for yards gained in one game. On November 20, 1977, he gained 275 yards rushing in a single game. If a player gained that many yards during every game using today's NFL schedule, how many total yards would he gain in a season? *(Note: The NFL is now playing a 16-game season.)*

3. The Chicago Bears are one of the few teams in the NFL that has not set passing records in recent years. Some people say that Chicago did not have good quarterbacks in the 1980s, when most teams' passing records were set. However, Johnny Lujack holds the single-game passing record for Chicago; he passed for 468 yards on December 11, 1949. The Buffalo Bills, a team that has had good quarterbacks during the 1980s, have a team record of only 419 yards. How many more yards did Lujack pass for on his record day?

5. Kevin Butler, who kicked field goals for Chicago from 1985–1992, holds the career record for most field goals for the Bears. He kicked 172 field goals during his career. How many points did he score on field goals?

_____

6. George Halas was the owner of the Chicago Bears for many years. He also served as coach of the Bears. However, he did not coach every year that he owned the team. The following table shows the years he coached and his record during those years.

Coaches	Won	Lost	Tied
1920-29	84	31	19
1933-42	88	24	4
1946-55	76	43	2
1958-67	76	53	6

How many games did he win?

_____

Los Angeles Rams records

The Los Angeles Rams have a long, exciting history in the National Football League. Over the years they have had many famous players such as Norm Van Brocklin, Elroy *(Crazylegs)* Hirsch, Tank Younger, Merlin Olson, and famous pass rusher Deacon Jones. The table below shows some of the Rams' team records.

Record	Player, year(s)	Yards
Career rushing yards	Eric Dickerson, 1983–87	7245
Career passing yards	Roman Gabriel, 1962–72	22,223
Career receiving yards	Henry Ellard, 1983–92	8816
Season rushing yards	Eric Dickerson, 1984	*2105
Season passing yards	Jim Everett, 1989	4310
Season receiving yards	Crazylegs Hirsch, 1951	1425
Game rushing yards	Eric Dickerson, 1/4/86	248
Game passing yards	Norm Van Brocklin, 9/28/51	*554
Game receiving yards	Willie Anderson, 11/26/89	*336

*NFL record

1. Eric Dickerson played for the Rams from 1983 through 1987, a total of five seasons. How many yards did he gain on the average each season?

_____

2. Norm Van Brocklin's NFL and Ram record for yards passing in one game has been on the record books since 1951. Using this year's date, how long has his record lasted?

_____

3. Elroy "Crazylegs" Hirsch set his season receiving record in a 12-game season. How many average yards did he gain for each game in that season? How many yards would he gain today in a 16-game season?

_____

_____

4. Eric Dickerson's 1984 rushing yards gained is the NFL record. How many yards did Dickerson gain for the Rams during his other four seasons?

_____

5. Willie Anderson's individual game record for yards gained receiving is an exceptional number. If he could average that over all 16 games in an NFL season, how many yards would he gain on pass receptions?

_____

Challenge problem

Compare Willie Anderson's season figure from question 5 with the NFL record. *(Note: The season record was set by Charlie Hennigan of the Houston Oilers in 1961. During that season Hennigan gained 1,746 yards on pass receptions.)* If Willie Anderson had gained 336 yards a game during every game, would he have broken Hennigan's record? By how much would he have broken it? Can you see why Anderson's game record is such an exceptional figure?

_____

_____

_____

_____

Cleveland Brown heroes

The Cleveland Browns were first formed as part of the old All-American Football Conference in the 1940s. They were admitted to the NFL in 1950. Answer the following questions about Cleveland.

1. Cleveland won six conference titles and three league titles during their first six years in the league. During those six years they won 58 games. What was their average number of wins per year during those first six seasons, rounded to two decimal places?

2. Otto Graham was the quarterback for those Cleveland teams. He averaged 8.63 yards for each pass attempt in his career; this is still the NFL record. He attempted 1,565 passes. How many total yards did he gain in all of those attempts?

3. Actually, Graham gained 13,499 yards passing, and his actual yards per attempt was 8.63555. What was the difference between your answer in problem 2 and his actual record? *(Note: This error was caused by rounding the 8.62555 to 8.63—which made your answer slightly larger than the real record.)*

4. Jim Brown was a running back for Cleveland from 1957 through 1965. When he retired, he held virtually every NFL career rushing record. He gained 12,312 yards in the nine years he played. Walter Payton of the Chicago Bears finally broke Brown's record in the 1980s. Payton gained a total of 16,726 yards rushing. How many more yards did Payton gain than Jim Brown? *(Note: Payton played longer—13 years.)*

5. Jim Brown gained his 12,312 yards in nine seasons. Payton gained his 16,726 yards during 13 seasons. Who gained more yards on the average per season? *(Note: Jim Brown played fewer games per season.)*

Cincinnati Bengals history

The Cincinnati Bengals were formed in 1968 as an expansion team in the AFL. Paul Brown, the coach of the Cleveland Browns during the 1950s, was a part owner and coach of the Bengals. He coached the Bengals for eight years, compiling a record of 55-59-1. He won eight games and lost six games in the team's third season. They won the Central Division title that year, making the playoffs for the first time. They lost to the eventual Super Bowl Champion, Baltimore, by a score of 17-0. Sam Wyche, who coached the Bengals from 1984-91, won the most games as head coach of the Bengals. His record is 64 wins and 68 losses. He took Cincinnati to Super Bowl XXIII, where they lost to San Francisco by a score of 20 to 16.

1. How many points were scored in Super Bowl XXIII?

_____

2. What was the total number of games that Paul Brown coached for the Bengals?

_____

3. If Paul Brown won a total of 170 games, how many games did he win with other teams?

_____

4. How many more games did Sam Wyche coach for the Bengals than Paul Brown?

_____

5. How many years has Cincinnati had a team in the NFL?

_____

6. As of the 1992 season, Cincinnati had won 184 games in the NFL. How many games were won by coaches other than Paul Brown and Sam Wyche?

_____

Indianapolis Colts history

The Indianapolis Colts did not always play in Indianapolis; in fact, they had a much longer history as the Baltimore Colts. Therefore, many of their team records are held by players who played in Baltimore.

1. The most famous Colt of all was Johnny Unitas, the quarterback who played for Baltimore from 1956-1972. During his 17 years in the NFL, "Johnny U" passed for 39,768 yards. How many yards gained passing did he average during each of those 17 years?

2. Colt quarterback Jeff George completed 167 passes during 1992. His average gain per completion was 11.75 yards. How many total yards did he gain on his passes during the 1992 season?

3. Did Jeff George pass for more yards in 1992 than Johnny U's average year? Or was Johnny U's average better? Whose was better, and by how much?

4. Rohn Stark, the Colts' punter, is one of the best punters in the NFL. In 1992 he punted 83 times, for a total of 3,716 yards. How long was his average punt? (Any average over 40 yards is considered to be good.)

5. Raymond Berry was a wide receiver for the old Baltimore Colts; he was the favorite receiver of Johnny Unitas. He still holds the Colts' season record for pass receiving yardage; in 1960 he gained 1,298 yards catching passes in a 12-game season. How many yards did he average for each of the 12 games?

Silver and black attack

George Blanda, who finished his career with the old Raiders, Oakland played longer than any other player in the NFL. Consider a list of his accomplishments:

1. George played in 348 games in his career, which began in 1949 with the Chicago Bears and ended in 1975 with the Oakland Raiders. Jim Marshall, who played for Cleveland and Minnesota, is second on the list of games played. He appeared in 282 games. How many more games did George Blanda play?

_____

2. Blanda was a quarterback who also was a place kicker. With 2,002 points, he holds the all-time record for points scored. Jan Stenerud, a kicker for Kansas for most of his career, is second on the scoring list with a total of 1,699 points. How many points did the two players score together?

_____

3. Bo Jackson, who played some football with the Los Angeles Raiders, still holds the team record for most yards gained in one game. He gained 221 yards in one game during the 1987 season. If he gained that same number of yards during all 16 games of the season, how many yards would he have gained?

_____

4. Eric Dickerson holds the NFL record for most yards gained during one season when he played for the Los Angeles Rams. He gained 2,105 yards rushing during the 1984 season. How many more yards would Bo Jackson have gained if he had rushed for 221 yards during every game of a season?

_____

Challenge question

Blanda scored his 2,002 points with nine touchdowns and 335 field goals. How many extra points did he make? (*Remember: The individual who scores a TD is only credited with six points.*)

_____

Halftime munchies

Examine the following menu. Then find what your bill would be for each meal purchased at the stadium. Remember that you may have to make several calculations to find the answer.

Menu	
Hot dogs	$2.00
Polish sausage dog	$3.00
Nachos	$2.50
Pizza (slice)	$2.00
Small soft drink	$1.00
Medium soft drink	$1.50
Large soft drink	$2.00
Souvenir cup	$3.00
Large coffee	$1.00

3. When Don went to get something to eat, the score was Kansas City 24, Denver 14. There was a long line at the concession stand. When he got back, Denver was ahead by three points. Kansas City did not score while he was gone. Find the total number of points on the scoreboard when Don came back to his seat.

1. Mary Jo bought two hot dogs, a small soft drink, and two medium drinks. How much was her total purchase?

2. David bought a Polish sausage dog, two orders of nachos, and a large soft drink. He ate it all so fast he felt terrible for the rest of the game. How much did he have to pay for the meal that made him feel so bad?

4. Karen went to buy food for everybody in her group. She insisted that they all buy the same thing because she couldn't remember seven different orders. So she bought seven hot dogs and seven small colas at the Concession Stand. How much did she spend in all?

5. Trisha had a ten-dollar bill for food. If she bought a Polish sausage dog, one order of nachos, and a souvenir drink, how much change did she receive?

All-purpose yards leaders

An interesting new statistic that is being kept for football players is "all-purpose yards gained." This statistic is kept for players who may carry the ball, catch passes, return punts, or return kickoffs. David Palmer, who played for Alabama during the early 1990s, is one player who performed any or all of these plays. Probably the most famous player who did all of these was Raghib "Rocket" Ismail, who played for Notre Dame in the late 1980s.

Use the information presented in the following problems to compute the "all-purpose yards gained" statistic for each of the players described in the problem. Remember that you may have to make several computations to find the total yards gained.

1. "Flash Frederickson" averaged nine yards per carry for 14 running plays. He also returned a kickoff for 38 yards and caught two passes for a total of 67 yards. How many all-purpose yards did Flash gain in this ball game?

2. "Stonehands" Harrison is a wonderful football player, but they call him "Stonehands" because he fumbles a lot. Last week "Stonehands" had an average game. He gained 123 yards running, caught two passes for 42 yards, and returned three kickoffs for exactly 24 yards each time. How many all-purpose yards did Stonehands gain that day? (Unfortunately, it was an average game; he also had four fumbles!)

3. Jimmy "The Flea" Flicker is a little player who is very fast. He caught five passes for an average of 18 yards, returned six punts for an average of 23 yards, and returned two kickoffs for an average of 42 yards. How many all-purpose yards did he gain?

Challenge problem

Can you find statistics on how many all-purpose yards a player gained in a college or professional football game that occurred this year?

College quarterback ratings

The quarterback position is so important for a football team. How do you tell who is the best quarterback? People who create football statistics have tried different ways of rating passers to give some comparative indication of their ability. But many things can happen when a quarterback throws the ball, so the statistical formulas are rather complicated.

      The formula for rating college quarterbacks is shown below. An example is provided to help you work your way through the statistic; a second problem is given for you to do on your own.

Wild Willie Wilson's passing statistics for last year:

Passes completed:	143
Passes attempted:	251
Yards gained:	1,543
Passing touchdowns	21
Interceptions	10

Step 1: The pass completions are divided by the attempts; the answer is multiplied by 100.

    143/251 = .5697 x 100 = 56.97

Step 2: The yards gained passing are divided by the attempts; the answer is multiplied by 8.4.

    1543/251 = 10.79 x 8.4 = 90.636

Step 3: The number of touchdowns is divided by the attempts; the answer is multiplied first by 100 and then by 3.3.

    21/251 = .08366 x 100 = 8.366 x 3.3
       = 27.609

Step 4: The interceptions are divided by the attempts; the answer is multiplied by 100 first and then by 2.

    10/251 = .0398 x 100 = 3.984 x 2
       = 7.968

Finally, add the answers for steps 1, 2, and 3; then subtract the answer for step 4.

$$56.97 + 90.636 + 27.609 = 175.215 - 7.968 = 167.247$$

So, Wild Willie Wilson's rating is 167.247. This statistic is calculated to make 100 the average score for quarterbacks. So, Wild Willie is an above-average quarterback. In fact, he looks to be a very good quarterback.

Now, try this statistic one more time. To the right you will find the statistics for Sad Sam Smith. *(Hint: You might guess from Sam's nickname that he is a below-average quarterback!)*

Passes completed:	*98*
Passes attempted:	*211*
Yards gained:	*843*
Passing touchdowns	*8*
Interceptions	*19*

Forward and backward

Figuring an offensive team's total yardage gained is not just a case of adding up the numbers. Players make positive plays, such as yards gained rushing and yards gained passing. But they also make negative plays, such as yards lost rushing or yards lost on a quarterback sack. There are also penalties; they work both ways. Examine the following game situations and figure the total yards gained by the team.

1. The East Side Buffaloes gained 256 rushing yards in a game. They also lost four yards on one play. The quarterback threw for 154 yards, but he was sacked seven times. He lost a total of 53 yards on the sacks. How many total yards did the Buffaloes gain?

2. In one game the Southside Stinkers gained 187 yards rushing and 458 passing. But they had 211 yards of penalties against the offense. How many total yards did they gain that night?

3. The Boise Bullets are a passing team. They ran for only 47 yards last night, but they passed for 398. They lost 38 yards on sacks, and they had three offensive penalties against them for a total of 25 yards. How many total yards did they gain last night?

4. The Lamont Lame Ducks didn't win a game from 1991 through 1993, but last night they did win. The Lame Ducks only gained 75 yards passing and 62 yards rushing, but their opponent had 165 yards in defensive penalties. When you count all of their yards and all of the penalty yards, how many yards did the Lame Ducks gain? *(Even after all of those gift yards, the Lame Ducks only won by two points!)*

5. Marta Lane, the principal at Horseshoe Bend High School, was trying to explain why they won a game so easily. She knew her team had run for 387 yards and passed for 256 yards. She also knew that they had been sacked only one time for a loss of seven yards, and only one penalty had been called against the offense for just five yards. But she didn't know how to figure the total yardage gained, so she simply said, "We marched up and down the field all night." Can you help Marta figure the total yards gained by her team that night?

6. Bob's favorite team was run out of the park last Saturday. They gained only seven yards rushing and 46 yards passing. They were penalized six times for 40 yards and they lost 72 yards when the quarterback was sacked nine times. What was the total yardage figure for Bob's team? *(Is it possible to find an answer to this problem? How would you explain it?)*

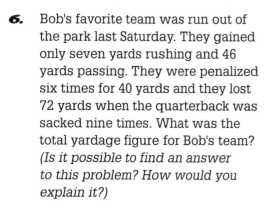

Football fashions

A large number of people watch football games. They pay a lot of money to attend each game. Teams need to attract large crowds, because it costs a great deal of money to put a football team on the field. For example, the Louisville Tigercats, which has 35 team members, paid the following equipment prices in 1955. *(Equipment costs more now!)*

Football equipment prices

1955 catalog

Equipment	Unit price	Needed	Total
Helmet	$35	35	
Shoulder pads	28	35	
Hip pads	18	35	
Thigh pads	4	70	
Knee pads	3	70	
Shoes	45	35	
Jersey	18	90	
T-shirt	8	90	
Pants	26	90	
Belt	5	35	
Socks (pairs)	2	92	

1. What is the total cost for each item, given the quantity of each item that the Tigercats needed?

2. The Tigercats bought more than one jersey for each player, because jerseys are torn during the games. If one-third of the Tigercat jerseys were torn during the season, how much did it cost to replace them?

3. One-seventh of the Tigercats' shoulder pads were broken due to hard hitting. How much will it cost to replace them?

_____

4. The Tigercats wore out three-quarters of their socks. How much will it cost to replace them?

_____

5. One-fifth of the Tigercat helmets were damaged so badly that they had to be thrown away. How many helmets did the Tigercats have left after the season?

_____

6. One-fifth of the Tigercats' uniform pants and one-seventh of their hip pads needed to be replaced after the season was over. What was the cost for these replacements?

New York Jet records

Solve the following problems.

1. Pat Leahy holds most of the New York Jet career kicking records. He kicked a total of 304 field goals, a Jet record. He also scored 1,470 points over his career, also a Jet career record. Using these figures, can you find how many extra points Leahy kicked?

2. Joe Namath is probably the New York Jets most famous player. He also holds many team records. In 1967 he threw 26 touchdown passes, a team record. If he also ran for three touchdowns that year, how many total points was he responsible for in 1967?

3. Don Maynard, who played for the Jets from 1960–1972, holds the Jets' record for total career touchdowns scored; he is also the co-holder of the season touchdowns scored record. If his record for a career is 88 touchdowns, and he scored 14 of them during the year 1965 in which he set the season record, how many points did he score on his touchdowns for all of the other years he played?

4. Actually, three different players are tied for the Jets record for TDs scored in a single season. Art Powell *(1960)*, Don Maynard *(1965)*, and Emerson Boozer *(1972)* all scored 14 TDs in the seasons shown. How many points did these players score together?

5. Wesley Walker, a Jet receiver in the 1980s, holds the Jet record for TDs scored in one game. He scored four touchdowns on September 21, 1986. That also gave him the record for the most points scored in one Jet game. How many field goals would the place kicker have to make in a game to tie Walker's record for most points scored in a game?

Buffalo Bill records

Solve the following problems.

1. The Buffalo Bills play their games in Rich Stadium; it holds 80,290 people. Their single-season attendance record was established in 1991, when 635,899 people attended the eight games held at Rich Stadium. If every single game had been sold out, how many more people could have come to the games?

2. O. J. Simpson holds three Bills records: career rushing yards, single-season rushing yards, and single-game rushing yards. On November 25, 1976, he ran for 273 yards in a single game. If he had continued at this pace for all 14 games played in a season that year, how many would he have gained? By how much would he have broken his season record? *(Note: his season record is 2,003 yards gained in one year, 1973.)*

3. Scott Norwood, who kicked for the Bills from 1985 through 1991, holds all of the career kicking records for Buffalo. He kicked 133 field goals and scored a total of 670 points. How many extra points did he kick?

4. Butch Byrd, who played defensive back for the Bills from 1964-1970, holds the all-time Bills record for interceptions. He intercepted 40 passes during the seven years that he played for the Bills. Assume that the other teams would have scored 12 field goals and nine touchdowns on their drives if Byrd had not intercepted the passes. *(The other times they would have punted the ball.)* How many points did he prevent with his interceptions?

5. Joe Ferguson holds the career passing records for Buffalo; he passed for 27,590 yards during his career from 1973-1984. Jim Kelly holds the single-season record; he passed for 3,844 yards in 1991. At that rate, how many years would it take Kelly to break Ferguson's record?

Detroit Lion records

Solve the following problems.

1. During recent seasons, Detroit has used a one-back running offense to feature the all-star running back, Barry Sanders. In the 1992 season Detroit gained a total of 1,644 yards rushing. Sanders gained 1,352 of those yards; five other backs combined to gain the remaining yards. What was the average number of yards gained by those five other backs?

2. Barry Sanders holds the single-season rushing record for Detroit; he gained 1,548 yards rushing in a 16-game season in 1991. Pat Studstill, who is now a TV announcer for NFL games, holds the single-season pass receiving record. He gained 1,266 yards on passes during the 14 games of the 1966 season. How many more yards did Sanders average per game than Studstill? *(Why are the answers so close?)*

3. Bobby Layne, a famous Detroit quarterback from the 1950s, holds Detroit's career record for passing with 15,710 yards gained over nine seasons. Gary Danielson holds the single-season passing yardage record with 3,223 yards gained in 1980. How much higher is Danielson's figure than Bobby Layne's average yards gained figure for the nine years he played?

4. Barry Sanders scored 17 TDs in 1991, giving him Detroit's record for most touchdowns scored in one season. Eddie Murray holds Detroit's record for most field goals scored in one season; he kicked 27 field goals during the 1980 season. How many more points did Sanders score on his TDs than Murray on his field goals?

5. Detroit's indoor stadium, the Silverdome, holds 80,500 people. Unfortunately, the team has not won many games there. In 1992 542,402 people attended Detroit games. Since they played eight games at home that season, how many more people could have attended the Detroit games?

Dallas Cowboy Super Bowls

Here is a chart that shows the final scores and the opponents for all of the Dallas Cowboys' Super Bowl games.

Bowl	Winner	Score	Opponent	Score	Winner	Loser
SB V	Baltimore	16	Dallas	13	$15,000	$7,500
SB VI	Dallas	24	Miami	3	15,000	7,500
SB X	Pittsburgh	21	Dallas	17	15,000	7,500
SB XII	Dallas	27	Denver	10	18,000	9,000
SB XIII	Pittsburgh	35	Dallas	31	18,000	9,000
SB XXVII	Dallas	52	Buffalo	17	36,000	18,000
SB XXVIII	Dallas	30	Buffalo	13	36,000	18,000

Solve the following problems

1. The Dallas Cowboys have played in the Super Bowl seven times, more than any other team. They played their first Super Bowl game in 1971. They played Baltimore and lost. They played against Buffalo in 1993 and 1994 and won both games. How many years were there between Dallas's first Super Bowl game and their 1994 game?

2. How many total points has Dallas scored in its Super Bowl games?

3. How many points have Dallas opponents scored in those same games?

4. What was the average number of points scored by Dallas? Their opponents?

5. Assume that Dallas had one coach for all of their Super Bowl games. How much would that coach earn for coaching in those Super Bowls?

6. If 48 Dallas players were given the winner's share, what was the total amount of money paid to the Dallas players?

Kansas City Chiefs history

The Kansas City Chiefs played their first game during the 1960 season as part of the old American Football League. Then known as the Dallas Texans, they played in Dallas for the 1960, 1961, and 1962 seasons before moving to Kansas City.

1. Kansas City has been involved in the two longest games in league history. The longest game was a playoff game against Miami on Christmas Day 1971. At the end of the game, the score was tied at 24 points. Neither team scored in the first overtime period. Miami finally made a field goal 7 minutes and 40 seconds into the second overtime period. If each quarter and the first overtime were 15 minutes long, what was the total length of that football game?

M I S S O U R I

2. In the second longest overtime game, the Dallas Texans were playing the Houston Oilers in the 1962 AFL championships game. The wind was blowing very hard. Dallas won the coin toss and wanted to take the wind at their back. The captain made a mistake, however, and Houston got both the ball and the wind. But Houston did not score in the first overtime. Dallas then got the wind in the second overtime, and they kicked a field goal 2 minutes and 54 seconds into the second overtime. What was the total length of that game? *(Again, each quarter and the first overtime period were 15 minutes long.)*

3. Kansas City also played in the first Super Bowl, where they met the Green Bay Packers on January 15, 1967. Green Bay won the game, 35 to 10. If only one field goal was kicked during the game, what was the total number of TDs scored by both teams?

4. Three years later, in 1970, Kansas City returned to the Super Bowl and defeated the Minnesota Vikings 23 to 7. Minnesota threw three interceptions and lost two fumbles. If all of those Minnesota possessions might have resulted in touchdowns, what was the maximum number of points that Kansas City prevented with the turnovers?

Pre-game pep

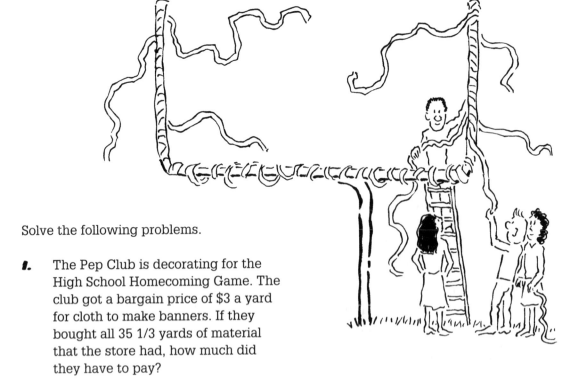

Solve the following problems.

1. The Pep Club is decorating for the High School Homecoming Game. The club got a bargain price of $3 a yard for cloth to make banners. If they bought all 35 1/3 yards of material that the store had, how much did they have to pay?

_____

2. Club members cut the 35 1/3 yards of cloth into banners that were two-thirds of a yard long. How many banners did they make?

_____

3. Jeff and Juanell were in charge of making signs. They each got a piece of paper from the office; Juanell's was 4 2/3 yards long and Jeff's was 3 1/2 yards long. If they combined their paper to make a longer sign, how long would it be all together?

_____

4. Sam cut 5 1/3 yards of crepe paper into strips that were 3/4 of a yard long. After he was finished he decided that he needed more strips, so he got another 5 strips from LaShonda. How many strips did he have when he was done?

_____

5. Karen had 15 1/2 yards of streamers. She used half of it to make one decoration. Then she used 2 1/3 yards for another decoration. How much of her original piece of material is left?

_____

Crazy college capers

Solve the following problems

1. On November 12, 1955, a raging storm blew across the rolling hills of eastern Washington. Unfortunately, Washington State University had scheduled a game with San Jose State that afternoon. It was cold and snowy, and a fierce wind blew. The game went on anyway. Although 412 students came to see the game, none actually made a move to buy a ticket. Finally, one lonely fan bought a ticket to see the day's contest. After that, the ticket sellers should have gone home. No one else bought a ticket that day—a good thing, because it snowed over a foot during the game, making visibility poor. It was difficult to tell if a player had made a first down or not. Did it matter? No. The game ended in a 13–13 tie. How many more points were scored than tickets sold?

2. During the Cotton Bowl in 1954, the Rice Owls were playing the Alabama Crimson Tide. The Owls had the ball, deep in their own territory at their own five-yard line. The quarterback pitched the ball to Dickie Moegle, the star Rice halfback. Moegle broke free around the right end. He was off to the end zone, 95 yards away. He was running free down the Alabama sideline. He was past the last Alabama player; he would score! Suddenly Tommy Lewis, an Alabama captain, was there, without a helmet. He made a beautiful open field tackle at the Alabama 41-yardline. There was just one problem. Lewis was not on the field for this play. He had run from the bench to make the touchdown-saving tackle! The referees huddled. What should they do? Lewis obviously should be called for a penalty. Their decision: Moegle was running free; the rules state that he should be awarded a touchdown. A player cannot come off the sideline to illegally participate in a play. How far did Moegle actually run with the ball?

3. The most famous mix-up in football occurred in 1982 during the final seconds of the Stanford-California season-ending game. Stanford quarterback John Elway had just directed a scoring drive; Stanford was ahead 20 to 19 with only four seconds left to play. All Stanford had to do was kick off and tackle the runner, and the game would be over—a tremendous "comeback" win engineered by John Elway. But Stanford kicked short to prevent a runback. Kevin Moen caught the ball, starting forward. He was surrounded. He lateraled the ball to a teammate. That player was surrounded. He lateraled to another teammate just before being tackled. The clock reached zero. The Stanford fans cheered. The Stanford band started marching out of the end zone onto the field. But the ball was still live. A final lateral put the ball back in Kevin Moen's hands. He ran into the Stanford band. Was he tackled? Almost. By whom? A Stanford trombone player in the end zone! California had scored the winning TD, with the help of Stanford's band. California's best blockers were the Stanford band members. What was the final score?

Wheeling and dealing

During the 1980s the San Francisco 49ers were the hottest team in the NFL. They won four Super Bowls during that decade. Here are some interesting facts about the 49ers.

1. On October 14, 1990, the San Francisco passing attack was working at its best. Joe Montana set the 49er record that day for TD passes, throwing for six touchdowns. Jerry Rice, the 49er receiver, caught five of the touchdown passes. How many points were scored by other 49er receivers that day?

2. In 1992, Jerry Rice scored 1 rushing TD and 10 receiving TDs. Ricky Watters scored nine rushing TDs and two receiving TDs. How many points did each of them score?

3. Late in the 1993 season, or early in the 1994 season, Jerry Rice will probably break the all-time scoring record for touchdowns set by Jim Brown. Brown scored 126 TDs in his career. At the end of the 1992 season, he had scored 108 touchdowns. How many more points must he score to break Brown's all-time record?

4. Roger Craig, the 49er running back who holds the team record for most yards rushing in one season, had some of his best days against the Denver Broncos. He gained 417 yards rushing in just four games against the Broncos. On the other hand, he gained only 72 yards in three games against the Pittsburgh Steelers. How much better was his average rushing mark against the Broncos than against the Steelers?

5. In 1992, Steve Young led all NFL quarterbacks in the efficiency rating statistics. He ran for 537 yards and passed for 3,465 yards. Since he was injured briefly, assume that he played in 13 complete games. What was his combined average for both rushing and passing for each of those games?

Frantic fans

1. Jeri and Barbara collect football cards. Jeri tried to give Barbara one card so they will both have the same number of cards. But Barbara said, "No. I will give you your card back and one of my cards." Now Jeri has twice as many cards as Barbara. How many cards did each begin with?

2. The sixth-grade San Diego Chargers' Fan Club at Coral Ridge Elementary School collected dues from all of its members. The club collected $2.89. If each club member paid the same amount, and each club member paid that amount with five coins, how many nickels did the club receive?

How big is the team?

1. Prescott is a small high school. The Prescott Tigers have 15 players for offense and 16 players for defense. However, five players play both offense and defense. How many players are on the Prescott Tigers football team?

2. The Cougars are from a very large high school. Their offensive team has 34 players, their defensive team has 42 players, and their special teams have 24 players. However, 11 players play both offense and defense, 10 players play defense and special teams, and six players play offense and special teams. Three players are on all three squads. How many players are on the Cougars?

Rapid runners

1. The Tigers play an eight-game season. After three games in the season, Cesar has gained 387 yards running with the football. Is he on pace to gain 1,000 or more yards rushing for the season?

_____

2. During his junior year, Jorge ran for 758 yards. In his senior year he rushed for 1,093 yards. What was his percentage improvement from his junior to his senior year?

_____

Winner's edge

1. Maria challenged Bob to find how many games the Denver Broncos won during the 1980s. They played in the Super Bowl several times during the 80s, she said, so they had a good team. Then she gave Bob the following clues to find the number:

a. It is an odd number.
b. It is greater than 9 x 9.
c. The sum of the numeral's digits is an even number.
d. It is a multiple of 3.
e. It is less than 99.

Can you help Bob answer Mary's tricky question?

2. The final score for a college game was Cougars 19, Bruins 14. Football teams can score:

2 points for a safety or for a two-point conversion
3 points for a field goal
6 points for a touchdown with a missed extra point
7 points with a touchdown and an extra point

List all of the possible combinations that could have made a final score of 19 to 14. Then pick two of the combinations that you think are most likely and explain why.

Defensive delights

1. Defensive coaches keep track of the number of defensive tackles made by each player. They have developed a scoring system to help describe how each player did during a game. Defenders are awarded two points for a solo tackle and one point for an assisted tackle. If Dave the defensive tackle earns 16 points, and had twice as many assists as solo tackles, how many points did he earn for tackles and for assisted tackles?

2. Tank the Tackle can't remember his number. All he knows is that the sum of the digits of his number forms a prime number, which is the first digit of his number. What is his number? *(Hint: Defensive tackles can only wear numbers between 60 and 79.)*

Scoring schemes 1

1. Karl the Kicker scored 135 points last year. He kicked both field goals and points after touchdowns *(PATs)*. He scored four times as many points with field goals as he scored with PATs. How many field goals did he make; how many extra points did he make?

2. The Hokies scored seven times in their game with the Wahoos. They scored 33 points in all, making only TDs *(7 points)* and field goals *(3 points)* How many TDs and field goals did they score?

EMMITT SMITH

RODNEY HAMPTON

JOE MONTANA

TROY AIKMAN

JERRY RICE

ROCKET ISMAIL

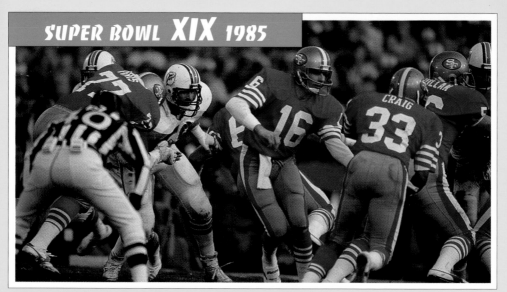

SUPER BOWL XIX 1985

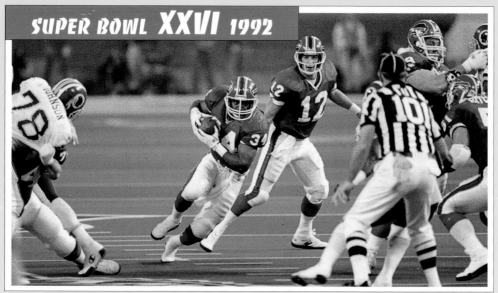

SUPER BOWL XXVI 1992

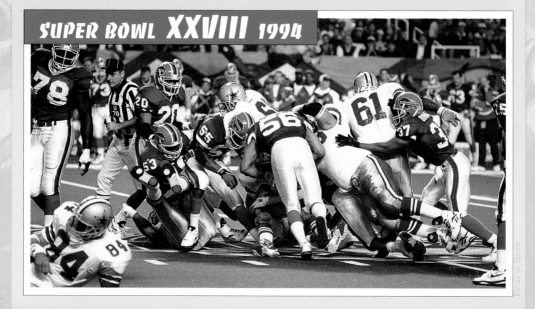

SUPER BOWL XXVIII 1994

Yearly rushing leaders

Year	Name, Team	Yards rushing
1992	Emmitt Smith, Dallas	1713
1991	Emmitt Smith, Dallas	1573
1990	Barry Sanders, Detroit	1304
1989	Christian Okoye, Kansas City	1480
1988	Eric Dickerson, Indiana	1659
1987	Charles White, LA Rams	1374
1986	Eric Dickerson, LA Rams	1821
1985	Marcus Allan, LA Raiders	1759
1984	Eric Dickerson, LA Rams	2105
1983	Eric Dickerson, LA Rams	1808

NFL Record: Eric Dickerson, 2105 Yards

Yearly passing leaders

Using the Professional Rating System

Year	Name, team	QB rating
1992	Steve Young, San Francisco	107.0
1991	Steve Young, San Francisco	101.8
1990	Jim Kelly, Buffalo	101.2
1989	Joe Montana, San Francisco	112.4
1988	Boomer Esiason, Cincinnati	97.4
1987	Joe Montana, San Francisco	102.1
1986	Tommy Kramer, Minnesota	92.6
1985	Ken O'Brien, NY Jets	96.2
1984	Dan Marino, Miami	108.9
1983	Steve Bartkowski, Atlanta	97.6

NFL Record: Joe Montana, 112.4

Yearly pass receiving leaders

Year	Name, team	Receptions
1992	Sterling Sharpe, Green Bay	108
1991	Haywood Jeffries, Houston	100
1990	Jerry Rice, San Francisco	100
1989	Sterling Sharpe, Green Bay	88
1988	Al Toon, NY Jets	93
1987	J. T. Smith, St. Louis	91
1986	Todd Christensen, LA Raiders	95
1985	Roger Craig, San Francisco	92
1984	Art Monk, Washington	106
1983	Todd Christensen, LA Raiders	92

NFL Record: Sterling Sharpe, 108 Receptions

Yearly scoring leaders

Year	Name, Team	Points scored
1992	Pete Stoyanovich, Miami	124
1991	Chip Lohmiller, Washington	149
1990	Nick Lowery, Kansas City	139
1989	Mike Cofer, San Francisco	136
1988	Scott Norwood, Buffalo	129
1987	Jerry Rice, San Francisco	138
1986	Tony Franklin, New England	140
1985	Kevin Butler, Chicago	144
1984	Ray Wersching, San Francisco	131
1983	Mark Moseley, Washington	161

NFL Record: Paul Hornung (1960), 176 Points

Yearly rushing leaders

Listed by yards per game

Year	Name, Team	Yards/Game	Total Yards
1992	Marshall Faulk, San Diego St.	163.0	1630
1991	Marshall Faulk, San Diego St.	158.8	1429
1990	Gerald Hudson, Oklahoma St.	149.3	1642
1989	Anthony Thompson, Indiana	163.0	1793
1988	Barry Sanders, Oklahoma St.	238.9	2628
1987	Ickey Woods, UNLV	150.7	1658
1986	Paul Palmer, Temple	169.6	1866
1985	Lorenzo White, Michigan St.	173.5	1908
1984	Keith Byars, Ohio St.	150.5	1655
1983	Mike Rozier, Nebraska	179.0	2148

NCAA record: Barry Sanders, 2628 Season rushing yards

Yearly passing leaders

Using passing efficiency ratings

Year	Name, Team	Passer Rating
1992	Elvis Grbac, Michigan	154.2
1991	Elvis Grbac, Michigan	169.0
1990	Shawn Moore, Virginia	160.7
1989	Ty Detmer, BYU	175.6
1988	Timm Rosenbach, Wash. St.	162.0
1987	Don McPherson, Syracuse	164.3
1986	Vinnie Testaverde, Miami	165.8
1985	Jim Harbaugh, Michigan	163.7
1984	Doug Flutie, Boston College	152.9
1983	Steve Young, BYU	168.5

NCAA record, Jim McMahon (BYU 1980), 176.9

Yearly receiving leaders

NCAA receptions per game

Year	Name, Team	Recept./Game	Total Recept.
1992	Sherman Smith, Houston	9.36	103
1991	Fred Gilbert, Houston	9.6	106
1990	Manny Hazzard, Houston	7.8	78
1989	Manny Hazzard, Houston	12.9	142
1988	Jason Phillips, Houston	9.8	108
1987	Jason Phillips, Houston	9.0	99
1986	Mark Templeton, LB State	9.0	99
1985	Rodney Carter, Purdue	8.9	98
1984	David Williams, Illinois	9.2	101
1983	Keith Edwards, Vanderbilt	8.8	97

NCAA record: Receptions in a game: 22 by Jay Miller of BYU, 11/3/73; Total per season: 142 by Manny Hazzard, Houston, 1989

Yearly scoring leaders

Year	Name, Team	Points/Game	Total Points
1992	Garrison Hearst, Georgia	11.5	1630
1991	Marshall Faulk, San Diego St.	15.6	1429
1990	Stacey Robinson, N. Illinois	10.9	1642
1989	Anthony Thompson, Indiana	14.0	1793
1988	Barry Sanders, Oklahoma St.	21.3	2628
1987	Paul Hewitt, S. Dakota St.	12.0	1658
1986	Steve Bartolo, Colorado St.	10.4	1866
1985	Bernard White, Bowl. Green	10.4	1908
1984	Keith Byars, Ohio State	13.1	1655
1983	Mike Rozier, Nebraska	14.5	2148

NCAA records: Game: 48 Points in one game, Howard Griffin (Illinois vs. S. Illinois), 9/22/90; Year: 234 points in a season, Barry Sanders (Oklahoma State) 1989

Helpful heroes 1

1. The Armadillos' quarterback, Toady Tom, is very fussy. He has to have exactly four cups of water halfway through a game. If Bill, the Armadillos' waterboy, only has containers that hold five cups and three cups respectively, how will he measure out four cups of water for Toady Tom to drink?

2. The Clemson Tiger mascot has a traditional job. After each Clemson score, the Tiger does the same number of push-ups as points his team has. *(Example: If Clemson scores a TD and leads 7-0, the Tiger does 7 pushups. If Clemson then scores a field goal to make the score 10-0, the Tiger then does ten more pushups, making a total of 17 pushups so far.)* This pattern goes on until the game is over. *(Note: The Tiger does not do six pushups for the TD and then seven for the TD and the extra point.)*

In one game during the early 1980s, Clemson scored 84 points on 12 touchdowns. How many pushups did the Clemson Tiger do that day?

Darrell's deeds

1. Darrell Green of the Washington Redskins is widely believed to be the fastest man in the National Football League. He runs a 40-yard dash in 4.2 seconds. How many "miles per hour" is that?

2. Darrell Green runs the 40-yard dash in 4.2 seconds. The record time for a miler to run a mile is approximately 3 minutes and 48 seconds. But if Darrell Green could keep up his pace for an entire mile, how long would it take him to run that mile? *(Of course, we all know that no human being can keep running that fast for an entire mile. But it is fun to see what his record would be.)*

Scoring schemes II

1. In 1992 the Seattle Seahawks came close to setting an all-time record for the lowest number of points scored. Let's imagine they managed to score ten points less than half as many points as the next lowest team, the New England Patriots. If New England had scored 186 points, how many would Seattle have scored?

2. Sudden Sam the Scoring Machine wanted to make a touchdown in every game. In half of the games he played, he scored three TDs. In one-quarter of the games, he scored two TDs. In one-sixth of the games, he scored just one TD. In three games he did not score. Please answer the following questions:

a. How many games did Sudden Sam play in all together?

b. How many TDs did he score in all?

c. What was the total number of points that he scored?

Helpful heroes II

1. The Warriors are traveling to play the Wildcats. A snowstorm was blowing as the Warriors left town. It took them 40 minutes at 20 miles an hour to drive through the storm. Then the bus had to make up lost time, so it traveled the last 100 miles at an average speed of 70 miles an hour on the freeway.

What was the average speed of the bus for the trip?

If they scheduled two hours for the trip, how many minutes were they early or late?

2. Carrie and Fred mixed caramel corn to sell in the concession stand. Because of a mix-up, they were given different recipes. Carrie's caramel corn was 70% popcorn and 30% peanuts, while Fred's was 60% popcorn and 40% peanuts. Together Carrie and Fred made a total of 30 pounds of caramel corn, and used 19 pounds of popcorn. How much caramel corn did Carrie make? How much did Fred make?

PROJECTS

Average salary

1. Salaries for football players were lower than those for players in other sports until 1993. A new free-agency rule in that year allowed football players to increase their salaries dramatically. Below you will find the average salary for each offensive football player.

Average salaries for starters at each position

1992 data

Offense		Defense	
Quarterbacks	$1,639,320	Defensive linemen	$661,065
Running backs	562,660	Linebackers	763,515
Wide receivers	682,115	Defensive backs	612,115
Tight ends	575,640	Kickers	349,440
Offensive linemen	570,965	Punters	302,120

Figure out the following. *(Suggestion: Since these are big numbers, you might like to use a calculator to help solve these problems.)*

a. What is the average salary needed to field an offensive football team?

_____

b. What is the difference between the highest average salary and the lowest average salary?

_____

c. What is the total cost for an average defensive line? Offensive line?

_____

d. The positions of quarterback, running backs, receivers, and tight ends have been called the "skill positions." What is the cost for an average team for the skill positions?

_____

e. What is the average salary for an offensive team? For a defensive team? (Note: Count the kickers as defensive players.) Why is one higher than the other?

_____

_____

_____

_____

Average quarterback salaries

Player	Above average	Below average
Dan Marino		
Steve Young		
Dave Krieg		
Bubby Brister		
Randall Cunningham		
Vinnie Testaverde		

1. Here are the names of five NFL quarterbacks. Do you think their salary would be above or below the average given for the quarterbacks? Write in your prediction for each player. Add a statement as to why you think the salaries would be above or below average.

_____

_____

_____

_____

_____

_____

_____

_____

2. Why do you think quarterbacks are the highest paid players?

_____

3. Why do you think punters are the lowest paid players?

_____

4. List other players at other positions and estimate if they are paid above or below the league averages.

_____

_____

_____

Quarterback statistics

American Football Conference

Leading passers, 1992 season

Player, team	Passes attempted	Passes completed	TDs	Interceptions
Warren Moon, Houston	346	224	18	12
Dan Marion, Miami	554	330	24	16
Neil O'Donnell, Pittsburgh	313	185	13	9
Jim Kelly, Buffalo	462	269	23	19

When we examine statistics, it is sometimes easy to jump to conclusions. For example, when you examine the statistical chart, you find that Neil O'Donnell threw the fewest interceptions, right? But he also threw the fewest passes. Is that important? Yes. One way to compare statistics is to change them to percentages so we get a comparison based upon 100. Then we are saying, "If they all threw 100 passes, what number would have been intercepted?" Using this number, we can compare the quarterbacks in a better manner.

1. Compute the percentage completion figure for each quarterback. *(Do this by comparing the number of completions and the number of passes attempted.)* Then rate them from top to bottom by that percentage.

2. Compute the percentage of interceptions to passes attempted for each quarterback. Then rate them from top to bottom by that percentage.

3. Compute the percentage of touchdowns to passes attempted for each quarterback. Then rate them from top to bottom by that percentage.

_____

_____

_____

_____

4. Now enter your numbers into the chart below.

Percent of passes that were

Quarterback	Completed	Intercepted	Touchdowns
Warren Moon			
Dan Marino			
Neil O'Donnell			
Jim Kelly			

5. Which quarterback do you think played the best? Why? Is there a right answer to this question?

_____

_____

_____

_____

_____

The price of victory

You are the business manager for your high school football team. You have won all your games to this point. It is now time to plan the trip to the state championship game. The athletic association has promised you they will help meet the expenses. Plan your budget. How much will you have to spend?

Note: You must provide for the expenses of 45 football players, six coaches, and three team managers. You must stay at a hotel for two nights before the game and one night after the game.

A. What do you HAVE to pay for?

_____

_____

_____

_____

_____

_____

_____

_____

_____

_____

_____

B. How much will each item cost?

$ _____

$ _____

$ _____

$ _____

$ _____

$ _____

$ _____

$ _____

$ _____

$ _____

$ _____

C. What is the final cost?

$ _____

You can solve this problem in two ways: 1.When you find what you need, ask an adult for estimated dollar figures. 2. It would be more interesting, however, to call or visit businesses in your area to see what the actual costs would be.

Here comes the Turk

An NFL team can keep 45 players on its active roster. That is not very many, when you consider that a coach must have offensive players, defensive players, and kicking specialists. Listed below are the positions that must be filled on an NFL team. (For simplicity, we have assigned the defensive team to play four down linemen and three linebackers.

Offensive positions	Defensive positions
Split end	Left defensive end
Left tackle	Left defensive tackle
Left guard	Right defensive tackle
Center	Right defensive end
Right guard	Left outside linebacker
Right tackle	Middle linebacker
Tight end	Right outside linebacker
Quarterback	Left corner
Running back	Free safety
Fullback	Strong safety
Wide receiver	Right corner
Place kicker	Punter

How many players should you keep for each position? Remember, you have a 45-man limit on the roster. Players do get hurt; you will need to have substitutes for every position. However, a substitute might play more than one position. Also, consider the following in making your choices:

a. Coaches like to keep three quarterbacks. If one gets hurt, it is difficult to hire a quarterback and teach him the offense in the middle of the year.

b. Coaches like to keep three tight ends. This gives them extra blockers for goal line plays.

c. Coaches like to have extra defensive backs to use in the "nickel" and "dime" packages. *(These terms describe having five or six defensive backs in the game playing for obvious passing situations.)*

d. No NFL team uses the same player for punting and place kicking.

1. During the summer, when teams are trying to cut players to get to the 45-player limit, make a list of all the players on your favorite team *(returning players, newly signed players, and new draft choices).* See if you can "help the coach" get down to the 45-player limit.

2. Watch for the new "salary cap." Use the salary information in these projects to see if your team can afford the players you select.

Weight-lifting exercises

Football players lift weights to build up their muscles and their weight. Over a season of lifting weights, the average player may move enormous amounts. Help "Walt the Weight Lifter" figure out what he lifts in a year.

1. Walt lifts weights all 52 weeks of the year.

2. Walt lifts weights 4 times a week.

3. Walt performs four lifts
    a. Bench press   210 pounds
    b. Incline press   170 pounds
    c. Squats   380 pounds
    d. Curls   80 pounds

4. Walt lifts the weights shown above each time for each lift.

5. Walt performs each lift 20 times.

Using the weights shown above for each of Walt's lifts:

a. How much weight does Walt move in a year for each lift?

_____

b. How much total weight does Walt move in a year with all of the lifts?

_____

c. How many weeks will it take Walt to join the "Million Pound Club" for all of his lifts put together? *(The "Million Pound Club" is an elite group of lifters who have all lifted at least one million pounds).*

_____

d. How many weeks will it take Walt to join the "Million Pound Club" for each lift?

_____

Since the numbers will be large, you may want to use a calculator to help you with the computations. Also, ask your coach, or read in a magazine, which muscles each of the weight lifts builds.

Weight-lifting sets

Tommy the Big Tackle, who plays for the Cougars, lifts weights in the off-season to keep his muscles strong. He follows the plan listed below.

Tommy does not want to hurt himself, so he practices with less than the total amount of weight he can lift. His practice schedule is shown below:

Set 1: He lifts 60% of his maximum load ten times. He repeats this set three times, with a short pause between each set of ten lifts.

Set 2: He lifts 70% of his maximum load six times. He repeats this set two times, with a short pause between each set of six lifts.

Set 3: He lifts 80% of his maximum load two times. This is done only once.

Tommy does each of these sets with his four different lifts. His lifts, and his maximum weight lifted for each lift, is shown below:

Bench Press   240 pounds
Incline Press 210 pounds
Squats   410 pounds
Curls   90 pounds

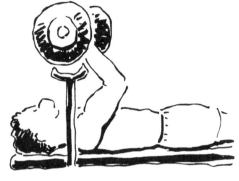

1. How much weight does Tommy practice with for Set 1? Set 2? Set 3?

_____

2. How much total weight does Tommy lift in Set 1? Set 2? Set 3?

_____

3. If Tommy lifts weights 6 days a week, how much weight does he lift in a week?

_____

4. All together, Tommy lifts weights 30 weeks of the year. How much total weight does he lift?

_____

5. How long will it take Tommy to join the "Million Pound Club?"

_____

Frequent flyer miles

Football teams travel an amazing number of miles over the years as they fly to play games. Consider the regular year schedule for two teams, one located in the center and one located in a corner of the country.

1993 schedule

	Chicago Bears			Seattle Seahawks	
Week 1	N.Y. Giants	Home		San Diego	Away
Week 2	Minnesota	Away		L.A. Raiders	Home
Week 3	Bye Week			New England	Away
Week 4	Tampa Bay	Home		Cincinnati	Away
Week 5	Atlanta	Home		San Diego	Home
Week 6	Philadelphia	Away		Bye Week	
Week 7	Bye Week			Detroit	Away
Week 8	Minnesota	Home		New England	Home
Week 9	Green Bay	Away		Denver	Away
Week 10	L.A. Raiders	Home		Houston	Away
Week 11	San Diego	Away		Cleveland	Home
Week 12	Kansas City	Away		Bye Week	
Week 13	Detroit	Away		Denver	Home
Week 14	Green Bay	Home		Kansas City	Home
Week 15	Tampa Bay	Away		L.A. Raiders	Away
Week 16	Denver	Home		Phoenix	Home
Week 17	Detroit	Home		Pittsburg	Home
Week 18	L.A. Rams	Away		Kansas City	Away

As you can see, each team plays eight home games and eight away games during the season, and has two weeks where they do not play. The question is, how far does each fly? The away sites are listed in the chart below, with the one-way distance between Chicago/Seattle and their opponents.

Chicago flies to:	Mileage	Seattle flies to:	Mileage
Minneapolis	304	San Diego	910
Philadelphia	589	Boston	2170
Green Bay	156	Cicinnati	1707
San Diego	1498	Detroit	1667
Kansas City	346	Denver	887
Detroit	196	Houston	1646
Tampa Bay	885	Los Angeles	829
Los Angeles	1517	Kansas City	1300

1. How far does each team fly during a season? *(Remember the distances shown are one-way mileages.)*

_____

_____

2. Who flies further?

_____

3. Figure out the time zone changes that each team has to go through on each trip. Who do you think has the easier travel schedule? Why?

_____

_____

_____

Tampa Bay vs. Green Bay records

Comparing team records is not always fair because some teams have been in the league longer than others. Here are some team records for the Green Bay Packers, a long-time NFL team, and the Tampa Bay Buccaneers, a team that joined the NFL in the 1970s. Compare the records:

Green Bay records*

Record category	Player, year	Record
Career rushing yards	Jim Taylor, 1958-66	8,207 Yds.
Career passing yards	Bart Starr, 1956-71	23,718 Yds.
Career receiving yards	James Lofton, 1976-86	9,656 Yds.
Career points	Don Hutson, 1935-45	823 Pts.
Seasonrushing	Jim Taylor, 1962	1,407 Yds.
Season passing	Lynn Dickey, 1983	4,458 Yds.
Season receiving	Sterling Sharpe, 1992	1,461 Yds.
Season points	Paul Hornung	*176 Pts.
Game rushing	Jim Taylor, 12/3/61	186 Yds.
Game passing	Lynn Dickey, 10/12/80	418 Yds.
Game receiving	Bill Howton, 10/21/56	257 Yds.
Game points	Paul Hornung, 10/8/61	33 Pts.

*NFL record

Tampa Bay records

Record category	Player, year	Record
Career rushing yards	James Wilder, 1981-89	5,957 Yds.
Career passing yards	Vinny Testaverde, 1987-92	14,820 Yds.
Career receiving yards	Mark Carrier, 1987-92	5,018 Yds.
Career points	Donald Igwebuike, 1985-89	416 Pts.
Season rushing	James Wilder, 1984	1,544 Yds.
Season passing	Dough Williams, 1981	3,563 Yds.
Season receiving	Kevin House, 1981	1,176 Yds.
Season points	Donald Igwebuike, 1989	99 Pts.
Game rushing	James Wilder, 11/6/83	219 Yds.
Game passing	Doug Williams, 11/16/80	486 Yds.
Game receiving	Mark Carrier, 12/6/87	212 Yds.
Game points	Jimmie Giles, 10/20/85	24 Pts.

Compare the records for each team. What do you see?

1. Are the Packers' career records higher? What are the dates of their records? Was Tampa Bay even in the league during those years?

2. Are the Packers' season records higher? Are the Packers' individual game records higher?

3. Only one record for these two teams is an NFL record. Why do you think Paul Hornung's record for points scored in a season was so high? (Hint: He was a runner and a kicker.)

Second-place seasons

Denver and Minnesota are two teams with interesting Super Bowl records. They had good teams for several years; they each played in four different Super Bowls. However, both teams lost all four of their games. Here are the statistics about those games.

Game	Winner	Score	Opponent	Score
SB IV	Kansas City	23	Minnesota	7
SB VIII	Miami	24	Minnesota	7
SB IX	Pittsburgh	16	Minnesota	6
SB XI	Oakland	32	Minnesota	14
SB XII	Dallas	27	Denver	10
SB XXI	N.Y. Giants	39	Denver	20
SB XXII	Washington	42	Denver	10
SB XXIV	San Francisco	55	Denver	10

Go to a library and look for information on these games. You may find the information in old newspapers, almanacs, or magazines. Then answer the following questions:

1. Both of these teams had famous quarterbacks during some of their games. Who were these quarterbacks?

_____   _____

2. Look at the game statistics. Were the games as lopsided as their scores?

_____   _____

a. Did Denver or Minnesota have a large number of turnovers that gave away points? In which games?

_____

_____   _____

b. Were Denver or Minnesota ever ahead in one or more
   of the games? Has Minnesota ever been ahead in a Super
   Bowl? Has Minnesota ever scored in the first half of a
   Super Bowl?

   _____

   _____   _____

c. What else can you find out about these games?

   _____

   _____

Note: In 1994 Buffalo joined the group by losing four Super
Bowls. Can you find records for all of Buffalo's losses?

75   *Second-place seasons*

Comparing passing teams

In recent years the Houston Oilers have become famous for using the "Run and Shoot" offense. This offense, despite its name, features the forward pass. Here are some statistics for Houston during the 1992 season, when their record was ten wins and six losses.

Leading rushers

Player	Carries	Yards gained	Longest	TDs
Team	353	1626	44	10
Lorenzo White, RB	256	1226	44	7
Warren Moon, QB	27	147	23	1
Gary Brown, RB	19	87	26	1
Cody Carlson, QB	27	77	13	1

Leading passers

Player	Attempts	Completions	Yards	TDs
Team	573	373	4231	27
Warren Moon, QB	346	224	2521	18
Cody Carlson, QB	227	149	1710	9

1. Houston had a thousand-yard rusher Who was he? Did New York? Who was he? Who gained more? What does this say about teams considered to be passing teams?

_____

_____

_____

2. Check the number of passing attempts and rushing attempts for Houston. Do the same for New York. Do these figures explain why one team is famous for passing and the other for running?

_____

Leading receivers

Player	Receptions	Yards	Longest	TDs
Team	373	4231	72	27
Haywood Jeffries, WR	90	913	47	9
Curtis Duncan, WR	82	954	72	1
Ernest Givins, WR	67	787	41	10
Lorenzo White, RB	57	641	69	1
Webster Slaughter, WR	39	486	36	4
Leonard Harris, WR	35	435	47	2

3. Check the number of passing yards gained and rushing yards gained for both teams. Do these figures explain why one team is famous for passing and the other for running?

_____

Comparing running teams

In recent years the New York Giants have been famous for using a hard-nosed, ball-control running offense. This offense has emphasized run first and pass second. Here are some statistics for New York during the 1992 season, when their record was six wins and ten losses.

Leading rushers

Player	Carries	Yards gained	Longest	TDs
Team	458	2077	63	20
Rodney Hampton, RB	257	1141	63	14
Jarrod Bunch, RB	104	501	37	3
Jeff Hostetler, QB	35	172	27	3
David Meggett, RB	32	167	30	0

Leading passers

Player	Attempts	Completions	Yards	TDs
Team	433	232	2628	14
Jeff Hostetler, QB	192	103	1225	8
Phil Simms, QB	137	83	912	5
Kent Graham, QB	97	42	470	1

Leading receivers

Player	Receptions	Yards	Longest	TDs
Team	232	2628	46	14
Ed McCaffrey, WR	49	610	44	5
David Meggett, RB	38	229	24	2
Rodney Hampton, RB	28	215	31	0
Mark Ingram, WR	27	408	34	1
Howard Cross, TE	27	357	29	2
Chris Calloway, WR	27	335	28	1
Stephen Baker, WR	17	333	46	2

1. Find the total number of offensive plays for both teams. Then: What percentage of the offensive plays were runs for both teams? What percentage of the offensive plays were passes for both teams?

3. New York plays two wide receivers and a tight end. How many total passes did these three receivers catch for New York? (Don't count the running backs.) Did the substitute receivers catch many passes?

2. Houston plays four wide receivers. How many total passes did the leading four wide receivers catch for Houston? (Note: Don't count the running back.) Did the substitute receivers catch many passes?

Comparing running teams

Professional statistics

Select your favorite professional football team. Then try to keep track of the statistics for the team for an entire season. You may want to consider the following:

1. Keep team statistics. Look at the statistical information presented in your paper for each game and decide what team statistics you would like to keep. Consider things such as the following:

2. Keep the same statistics for your opponent each week.

Offensive statistics:	Defensive statistics:	Combined statistics:
Points scored	Fumbles caused	Total penalties
Total first downs	Fumbles recovered	Penalty yardage
Running yardage	Passes intercepted	Kick off return yardage
Total number of running plays	Interception return yardage	Punt return yardage
Passing yardage	Tackles	
Passes attempted	Sacks	
Passes completed		
Passes had intercepted		
Total fumbles		
Fumbles lost		

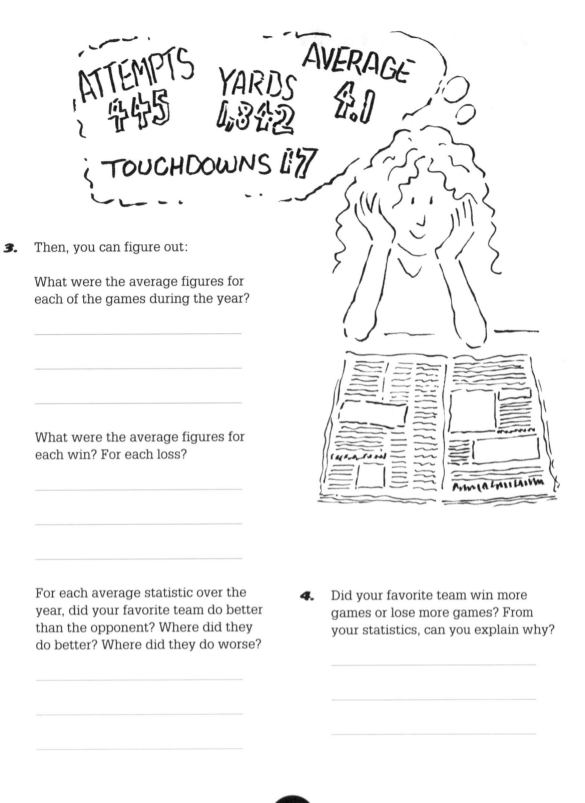

3. Then, you can figure out:

What were the average figures for each of the games during the year?

_____

_____

_____

What were the average figures for each win? For each loss?

_____

_____

_____

For each average statistic over the year, did your favorite team do better than the opponent? Where did they do better? Where did they do worse?

_____

_____

4. Did your favorite team win more games or lose more games? From your statistics, can you explain why?

_____

_____

_____

College statistics

Select your favorite college football team. Then try to keep track of the statistics for the team for an entire season. You may want to consider the following:

1. Keep team statistics. Look at the statistical information presented in your paper for each game, and decide what team statistics you would like to keep. Consider things such as the following:

2. Keep the same statistics for your opponent each week.

Offensive statistics:	Defensive statistics:	Combined statistics:
Points scored	Fumbles caused	Total penalties
Total first downs	Fumbles recovered	Penalty yardage
Running yardage	Passes intercepted	Kick off return yardage
Total number of running plays	Interception return yardage	Punt return yardage
Passing yardage	Tackles	
Passes attempted	Sacks	
Passes completed		
Passes had intercepted		
Total fumbles		
Fumbles lost		

3. Then, you can figure out:

What were the average figures for each of the games during the year?

_____

_____

_____

What were the average figures for each win? For each loss?

_____

_____

_____

For each average statistic over the year, did your favorite team do better than the opponent? Where did they do better? Where did they do worse?

_____

_____

4. Did your favorite team win more games or lose more games? From your statistics, can you explain why?

_____

_____

_____

BADGERS
HUSKIES
WILDCATS
TROJANS
BRUINS
TIGERS

Comparing statistics

Now that you have statistics for your favorite professional and college football teams, compare them. Then answer some of the following questions.

1. What is the average number of offensive plays for a professional team? For a college team?

_____

_____

2. What is the average number of running plays and passing plays for a college team? For a professional team?

_____

_____

3. What is the average number of points scored for both teams?

_____

_____

4. Can you find any relationships here? Does one team run more plays than the other? Do they score more points if they run more plays?

_____

_____

5. Who scores more of their points on touchdowns? Who scores more of their points on field goals? What kind of numbers will you have to work with to answer these questions?

_____

_____

6. What other questions can you ask and answer from the statistics you have compiled?

_____

_____

College quarterback stats

On pages 82-83, you learned how to figure the college passer's rating statistics. Let's review it one more time.

You need the following statistics from each game:

    Pass completions
    Pass attempts
    Yards gained passing
    Number of passing touchdowns
    Number of interceptions thrown

Then, make the following computations:

    Step 1 Divide the Pass completions by the Pass
            attempts; multiply answer by 100.

    Step 2 Divide the Yards gained passing by the Pass
            attempts; multiply answer by 8.4.

    Step 3 Divide Passing touchdowns by Attempts;
            multiply answer by 100 and then 3.3.

    Step 4 Divide Interceptions by Attempts; multiply
            answer by 100 and then 2.

    Step 5 Add answers from steps 1, 2, and 3; then subtract
            answer from Step 4.

Pick your favorite college quarterback. Find his statistics for each game during an entire season. Compute the statistic for each game, but compute it each week for his season totals. At the end of the year, you will have his passing rating for the entire year.

Suggestions:
Have some friends pick their favorite quarterback and compute his statistics.

Compare the passing ratings for each game. Whose favorite had the best day?

Compare the total passing rating score each week for your quarterbacks? Who is having the best season?

At the end of the year, compare your quarterbacks. Who had the highest final rating? Award that quarterback your own "Most Valuable Passer" award.

Who is the best kicker?

Kicking data for selected kickers

1992–93 season

| Kicker/team | Points | Kicks attempted/made | | | | |
		1-29 yards	30/39 yards	40/49 yards	50+ yards	Longest kick
Pete Stoyanovich	124	9/9	14/16	4/4	3/8	53
Morton Anderson	120	10/10	8/10	8/11	3/3	52
Lin Elliott	119	6/7	10/14	5/10	3/4	53
Steve Christie	115	11/11	3/6	7/8	3/5	54

If a team cannot score a touchdown, then it is vital that they make a field goal if they get close to the other team's goal. It is almost like "gift points" when a team scores a 50+-yard field goal, as it means the team scored points when it wasn't close to the other team's goal.

The chart above gives you some interesting statistics on four kickers who were among the leading scorers for kickers during the 1992-93 season. Examine the figures. Then pair off with a friend. Discuss these kickers in terms of the following:

a. Who was the best kicker from close range?

_____

b. Who was the best kicker from long range?

_____

c. Why do you think Stoyanovich had so many more attempts from long range?

_____

d. Who scored the most points on field goals?
(Remember the chart gives you total points, not field goal points.)

_____

e. Which kicker would you rather have if you were a coach? Why?

_____

_____

f. Who do you think is the best kicker? Is it the same person that you would like to have on your team? Why or why not?

_____

_____

_____

Kicking statistics for the season

Collect as many statistics as you can on several kickers who are kicking this year. Keep the statistics for an entire year. *(You may want to keep statistics for several kickers, as it is always possible that someone will be hurt and not kick very much during a year.)* Consider keeping the following statistics:

a. Number of kickoffs
b. Number of kickoffs kicked into the end zone for a touchback
c. Number of kickoffs returned for a touchdown
d. Average length of kickoff returns *(This is important: kickers who kick the ball high usually cause the other team to make shorter returns.)*
e. Number of field goals attempted and made
f. Number of point after touchdowns attempted and made
g. Number of field goals blocked
h. Number of point after touchdowns blocked
i. Length of all field goal kicks attempted and made
j. Any other statistic you think is important

Then show your statistics to a friend and discuss who is the best kicker.

The "games behind" statistic

The table below shows the team standings for an imaginary football league. The interesting statistics are in the "Games Behind" column. Let's examine it.

The Bruins are in the lead; therefore, the statistic is not figured for them. The Cardinals are in second place. Notice they have lost two more games and won two fewer games than the Bruins. As a result, if the Bruins lose their next two games and the Cardinals win their next two, the two teams will be tied. The "Games Behind" statistic tells you this number. It tells the number of Cardinal wins and Bruin losses that would result in a tie for first place.

Pioneer League football standings

Team	Wins	Losses	Ties	Games behind
Bruins	8	1	0	
Cardinals	6	3	0	2
Lions	5	4	0	3
Jets	4	5	0	4
Dogs	0	9	0	8

The first table is easy to read, because everyone has played the same number of games. That is not always true. Consider the following standings:

Pioneer League football standings

Team	Wins	Losses	Ties	Games behind
Bruins	8	0	0	
Cardinals	6	1	1	1 1/2
Lions	5	4	0	3 1/2
Jets	4	4	0	4
Dogs	2	5	1	5 1/2

This set of standings happens more often. Everyone has not played the same number of games. Two teams have played a tie game. How are those things figured?

Again, look at the Bruins and the Cardinals. The Bruins are in first place; the statistic is not figured for them. The Cardinals have won two less games than the Bruins, but they have lost 1 more. This puts the Cardinals 1 1/2 games behind the Bruins. They are two games behind in the win column, but only one game behind in the loss column. *(The tie does not help or hurt in figuring this statistic. However, at the end of the season when everyone has played the same number of games, it makes a major difference in who has the most victories or the most losses.)*

Follow your favorite team or teams for an entire season. Read the league standings in any newspaper. Be prepared to discuss how your team can win or lose the league title.

The "games behind" statistic

Records of AFC teams since the 1970 AFL/NFL merger*

Team	Wins	Losses	Ties	Pct.	Div. titles	Playoff berths	Post season record	Super Bowl record
Miami Dolphins	229	113	2	.669	10	14	16-12	2-3
L.A. Raiders	217	121	6	.641	9	14	17-11	3-0
Pittsburgh Steelers	203	140	1	.592	10	13	16-9	4-0
Denver Broncos	193	140	6	.570	7	9	9-9	0-4
Cleveland Browns	171	170	3	.501	6	9	3-9	0-0
Cincinnati Bengals	172	172	0	.500	5	7	5-7	0-2
Kansas City Chiefs	157	180	7	.466	1	5	5-7	0-0
Seattle Seahawks	121	139	0	.465	1	4	3-4	0-0
Buffalo Bills	157	185	2	.459	5	8	9-8	0-3
San Diego Chargers	151	188	5	.446	4	5	4-5	0-0
New England Patriots	153	191	0	.445	2	5	3-5	0-1
Houston Oilers	152	190	2	.444	1	9	7-9	0-0
N.Y. Jets	144	198	2	.422	0	5	3-5	0-0
Indianapolis Colts	144	198	2	.422	5	6	4-5	1-0

*Through 1992 season

These are the statistical records for all AFC teams since the 1970 merger. *(Please remember there were Super Bowls played before the official merger; that explains why the 1969 New York Jets' and Kansas City Chiefs' Super Bowls wins do not show in these statistics.)*

Part of the fun of watching football is keeping track of the statistics and then discussing what those statistics mean. To do this, you have to ask questions and find the answers in the chart. Consider:

1. How many AFC teams have never played in the Super Bowl during this time?

_____

_____

_____

_____

2. How many AFC teams have never played in the Super Bowl? *(To answer this question, you need to know that there were four Super Bowls played before the 1970 merger of the American and National Football Leagues. Those four Super Bowl teams were: Winners: Green Bay, two times, New York Jets, one time, and Kansas City Chiefs, one time. Opponents: Kansas City, Oakland Raiders, Baltimore Colts, and Minnesota Vikings. And you must also remember, of course, that the Oakland Raiders became the Los Angeles Raiders and the Baltimore Colts became the Indianapolis Colts.)*

_____

3. How many AFC teams have never played in a tie game? Who are they? *(Remember that since the league started allowing overtime games, the number of tie games has decreased dramatically.)*

_____

_____

_____

4. Which AFC team has played in the most Super Bowls? Which AFC team has won the most Super Bowls? Which AFC team has lost the most Super Bowls?

_____

_____

5. What is your favorite team? What is their record?

_____

_____

_____

6. For what other questions can you find answers in this table? Discuss these questions with a friend.

_____

_____

_____

Analyzing NFC records

Records of NFC teams since the 1970 AFL/NFL merger*

Team	Wins	Losses	Ties	Pct.	Div. titles	Playoff berths	Post season record	Super Bowl record
Washington Redskins	221	122	1	.644	5	13	18-10	3-2
Dallas Cowboys	215	129	0	.625	10	16	23-13	3-3
San Francisco 49ers	202	139	3	.592	12	13	17-9	4-0
Minnesota Vikings	201	141	2	.587	11	14	11-14	0-3
L.A. Rams	198	142	4	.582	8	14	10-14	0-1
Chicago Bears	179	164	1	.522	6	9	6-8	1-0
Philadelphia Eagles	163	175	6	.482	2	8	4-8	0-1
N.Y. Giants	158	184	2	.462	3	6	9-4	2-0
Detroit Lions	150	190	4	.442	2	4	1-4	0-0
Phoenix Cardinals	144	194	6	.427	2	3	0-3	0-0
Green Bay Packers	141	195	8	.421	1	2	1-2	0-0
New Orleans Saints	140	200	4	.412	1	4	0-4	0-0
Atlanta Falcons	138	202	4	.406	1	4	2-4	0-0
Tampa Bay Bucs	76	183	1	.294	2	3	1-3	0-0

*Through 1992

These are the statistical records for all NFC teams since the 1970 merger. *(Please remember there were Super Bowls played before the official merger; that explains why the 1967 and 1968 Green Bay Packer Super Bowl wins do not show in these statistics.)*

Part of the fun of watching football is keeping track of the statistics and then discussing what those statistics mean. To do this, you have to ask questions and find the answers in the chart. Consider:

1. How many NFC teams never played in the Super Bowl during this time?

_____

_____

_____

_____

2. How many NFC teams have never played in the Super Bowl? *(Remember that there were four Super Bowls played before the 1970 merger of the American and National Football Leagues. Those four Super Bowl teams were: Winners: Green Bay, two times, New York Jets, one time, and Kansas City Chiefs, one time. Opponents: Kansas City, Oakland Raiders, Baltimore Colts, and Minnesota Vikings. And you must also remember, of course, that the Oakland Raiders became the Los Angeles Raiders and the Baltimore Colts became the Indianapolis Colts.)*

_____

_____

_____

_____

3. How many NFC teams have never played in a tie game? Who are they? *(Remember that since the league started having overtime games, the number of tie games has decreased dramatically.)*

_____

_____

_____

_____

4. Which NFC team has played in the most Super Bowls? Which NFC team has won the most Super Bowls? Which NFC team has lost the most Super Bowls?

_____

_____

_____

5. What is your favorite team? What is their record?

_____

_____

6. For what other questions can you find answers in this table? Discuss these questions with a friend.

_____

_____

_____

_____

Comparing AFC/NFC records

Now that you have the charts on the records of all AFC and NFC teams since the 1970 merger, you can make comparisons between the two charts. Consider the following questions:

1. Who has the best record for the 22 seasons? Does that help explain why the coach became *(in 1993)* the coach with the most victories for a career?

_____

_____

2. Who has the worst record for the 22 seasons? Why?

_____

_____

3. What teams have never won a play-off game? Which conference are they in?

_____

_____

4. How many Super Bowls has each league won since the merger? *(Remember there were four Super Bowls played before the merger; each league won two and lost two.)*

_____

_____

5. Seattle and Tampa Bay have played fewer games than everyone else. Why? *(Hint: They were expansion teams.)*

_____

_____

6. Whose record should be getting better? Whose record is getting worse?

_____

_____

7. For what other questions can you find answers ? Discuss these questions with a friend.

_____

_____

8. These statistics include all seasons played from 1971 through 1992. Can you update the records after the 1993 season? Later seasons?

_____

_____

Miami's decade of champs

The University of Miami had an excellent record for the 10
seasons from 1983-92. Their record looks like this:

Season	Wins	Losses	Ties	National ranking
1983	11	1	0	1st—National champs
1984	8	5	0	18
1985	10	2	0	9
1986	11	1	0	2
1987	12	0	0	1st—National champs
1988	11	1	0	2
1989	11	1	0	1st—National champs
1990	10	2	0	3
1991	12	0	0	1st—National champs
1992	11	1	0	3

Questions to consider:

How many total wins did Miami have
during the decade?

_____

How many total losses did they have?

_____

What was their winning percentage for
the ten years?

_____

What other statistics might we collect?

_____

How many points did the team score each year?

_____

How many opponents points did they allow?

_____

How many TDs?

_____

How many field goals?

_____

How many safetys?

_____

Collect the same record for your favorite team. You might select a high school team, a college team, or an NFL team. The sports desk of your local newspaper can help you find the records for past seasons. Or, for college or professional teams, buy statistical record books that list the information.

Comparing your favorite teams

It is fun to compare records of your favorite teams with a friend. If you have different favorite teams, you can talk over about who has the best record or who is improving the most. Consider the following ten-year record for two professional teams, one from the American Football Conference and one from the National Football Conference.

Year	AFC: Cleveland Browns			NFC: Los Angeles Rams		
	Wins	Losses	Ties	Wins	Losses	Ties
1992	7	9	0	6	10	0
1991	6	10	0	3	13	0
1990	3	13	0	5	11	0
1989	9	6	1	11	5	0
1988	10	6	0	10	6	0
1987	10	5	0	6	9	0
1986	12	4	0	10	6	0
1985	8	8	0	11	5	0
1984	5	11	0	10	6	0
1983	9	7	0	9	7	0

You might wish to consider:

Who has the best ten-year record?

_____

Who has the best five-year record?

_____

What is the total number of wins for each team?

_____

What is the winning percentage for each team?

_____

You might like to discuss:

Who seems to be getting better? Which team's record seems to be getting worse?

_____

_____

What happens if you add 1993 statistics? How do the records change?

_____

_____

Can you add statistics from any later year? How do they affect the records?

_____

_____

Comparing teams and travel

On the following pages you will find these mileage charts:

      a. American Football Conference miles:
            The miles between each AFC city.

      b. National Football Conference miles:
            The miles between each NFC city.

      c. AFC - NFC miles:
            The miles between NFC cities and AFC cities.

Use the charts for the following:

1. Get this year's schedule for your favorite team. How far do they have to travel this year?

_____

2. Can you compare this year's travel to last year's travel schedule? Do they travel more miles? Fewer miles?

_____

3. Have a friend figure the miles his or her favorite team travels. Compare that to your team. Who has the more difficult travel schedule? Why?

_____

_____

4. Look at the time zone changes for each trip. How many times does your favorite team cross three time zones? two time zones? one time zone? No time zones? Make a chart that shows this information. Compare your chart to a chart showing the same information for your friend's team. Do you think it makes it more difficult to play when a team has to change three time zones?

_____

_____

5. Compare all the trips from all the charts:

What is the longest trip any team has to make?

_____

What is the shortest trip any team has to make?

_____

6. Compare your favorite team's winning record at home versus the winning record on the road. Does travel distance have anything to do with the road win/loss record? Does crossing more time zones have anything to do with the win/loss record?

_____

_____

_____

7. Does your favorite team play two games in a row on the opposite coast? Do they stay on that coast all week? Why or why not?

_____

_____

Note

All miles on the following charts are listed as International Air Nautical Miles. If you look in the dictionary, you will see there are three different types of mile measurements used. Statute miles are those highway miles that you see on highway signs. Nautical miles are longer than statute miles, used on the ocean by navies. International Air Nautical Miles are different still; they are the mileages used by pilots when they fly anywhere in the country or the world. The following shows the details:

Statute mile — 5,280 feet
Nautical mile — 6,080 feet
International air nautical mile —
  6,076.1155 feet

Miles between all NFC teams and all AFC cities

Team	Buffalo	Cincinnati	Cleveland	Denver	Houston	Indiana	Kansas City	LA Raiders	Miami	New England	NY Jets	Pittsburgh	San Diego	Seattle
Arizona Cardinals	1660	1356	1490	516	881	1285	907	329	1695	1994	1866	1578	272	964
Atlanta Falcons	628	330	483	1047	599	389	599	1692	498	830	667	458	1644	1899
Chicago Bears	415	231	261	775	822	148	346	1517	1028	754	643	371	1498	1495
Dallas Cowboys	1060	706	877	563	211	665	405	1075	959	1360	1211	933	1020	1445
Detroit Lions	220	200	81	972	945	194	534	1713	986	558	450	197	1693	1667
Green Bay Packers	424	295	292	766	875	216	367	1512	1097	765	666	407	1498	1453
Los Angeles Rams	1932	1651	1771	747	1209	1574	1191	*	2024	2271	2152	1866	92	829
Minnesota Vikings	650	533	541	595	933	446	356	1335	1308	984	903	657	1333	1205
New Orleans Saints	951	602	783	927	267	615	595	1456	570	1184	1022	790	1395	1814
New York Giants	259	514	383	1417	1241	580	962	2152	940	163	*	288	2127	2105
Philadelphia Eagles	239	442	328	1354	1159	514	896	2062	873	244	82	231	2038	2021
San Francisco 49ers	2011	1770	1866	838	1438	1688	1310	293	2237	2351	2249	1970	385	583
Tampa Bay Bucs	920	676	807	1317	682	740	911	1880	159	1033	877	752	1819	2195
Washington Redskins	255	359	279	1286	1059	438	819	2009	791	347	185	163	1979	2023

Miles from One NFC team to all other NFC cities

Team	Arizona	Atlanta	Chicago	Dallas	Detroit	Green Bay	LA Rams	Minnesota	New Orleans	NY Giants	Philadelphia	San Francisco	Tampa Bay	Washington
Arizona Cardinals	*	1372	1246	748	1439	1251	239	1108	1128	1866	1787	567	1552	483
Atlanta Falcons		*	534	634	525	603	1692	810	358	667	579	1861	352	532
Chicago Bears			*	701	196	70	1517	304	725	643	589	1605	885	1038
Dallas Cowboys				*	855	743	1075	758	390	1211	1131	1277	810	359
Detroit Lions					*	217	1713	462	799	450	402	1800	861	571
Green Bay Packers						*	1512	251	79	666	600	1587	955	2009
Los Angeles Rams							*	1335	1456	2152	2062	293	1880	820
Minnesota Vikings								*	918	903	862	1377	1158	838
New Orleans Saints									*	1022	941	1667	424	185
New York Giants										*	82	2239	877	103
Philadelphia Eagles											*	2147	806	1714
San Francisco 49ers												*	2077	2113
Tampa Bay Bucs													*	711
Washington Redskins														*

"Mileage between AFC and NFC Cities" from the Jeppesen 2 US (FP/LO) Low Altitude Flight Planning Chart. Copyright © 1987 Jeppesen Sandersen, Inc. Reproduced with permission of Jeppesen Sanderson, Inc.

Comparing teams and travel

Team	Buffalo	Cincinnati	Cleveland	Denver	Houston	Indianapolis	Kansas City	LA Raiders	Miami	New England	NY Jets	Pittsburgh	San Diego	Seattle
Buffalo Bills	*	362	153	1188	1129	395	754	1932	1020	341	259	171	1013	1848
Cincinnati Bengals		*	183	931	768	91	462	1651	810	656	514	229	1620	1707
Cleveland Browns			*	1033	949	213	583	1771	926	504	383	116	1748	1745
Denver Broncos				*	765	848	472	747	1475	1528	1417	1135	738	887
Houston Oilers					*	751	579	1209	817	1398	1241	982	1143	1645
Indianapolis Colts						*	383	1574	881	713	580	293	1547	1616
Kansas City Chiefs							*	1191	1069	1087	962	675	1165	1300
Los Angeles Raiders								*	2024	2271	2152	1866	92	829
Miami Dolphins									*	1087	940	858	1960	2353
New England Patriots										*	163	427	2250	2170
New York Jets											*	288	2127	2105
Pittsburgh Steelers												*	1840	1860
San Diego Chargers													*	910
Seattle Seahawks														*

Collecting trivia information

Many people are interested in sports trivia. Trivia questions deal with interesting, isolated facts that stump most people, but not the "trivia buffs." You can have a good time making up questions that your friends will have a tough time answering.

The following four pages include trivia questions for both college and professional teams, with both modern and historical questions.

1. Can you answer the questions? Can your mom or dad?

2. Can you stump your friends with these questions?

3. Can you make up more questions on your own?

4. Where can you get the information to make up trivia questions:

a. Try your library. They will have sports information books.

b. Try a bookstore in your town. They will have a sports section with sports reference books in them. You may also find record books that list records from different sports.

c. Keep a record of trivia information from your newspaper for an entire season. Then write questions about what you have collected.

Historical NFL trivia

1. Only two of the original fourteen teams who founded the NFL in 1920 have an unbroken history to the present. However, both teams have changed cities and one has changed its nickname. What two modern-day teams trace their origins to the 1920 season? How many years have they been in the NFL?

   _____

   _____

2. What is the team with the longest unbroken record of playing in one city with the same nickname? *Hint:* Their first year in the NFL was the 1921 season, and their record for that season was three wins, two losses, and one tie. How many years has this team been in the league?

   _____

   _____

3. Teams in the early years of the NFL did not play a regular schedule nor the same number of games. Several oddities occurred because of this fact in the first ten seasons of the NFL. For example:

   a. What team played the fewest number of games in the NFL? Did they win any games? How many games did they play?

   _____

   _____

b. What team played in both 1920 and 1921 before dropping out of the league, but played only a total of three games over the two seasons and lost them all?

   _____

c. What team played the most regular season games in the NFL? How many regular season games did they play? How many years ago? What was their final record for that year?

   _____

   _____

d. What was the original name of the NFL?

   _____

e. What 2 teams played the first game between two official NFL teams? What was the score? Who scored the first TD? What was the date?

   _____

   _____

4. Jim Thorpe, the famous Native American football player of the 1920s, was both the league president and an active player in 1920. What team did he play for?

   _____

Modern NFL trivia

1. Everyone knows that Dan Marino set the record for TD passes in one season, as he threw for 48 touchdowns in 1984. But what two players held the record for touchdown passes in a season before Marino? How many fewer points did their teams score than the Dolphins scored on Marino's passes?

_____

_____

2. Nine of the ten most watched TV programs _(those with the largest number of people watching their TV sets)_ were Super Bowls. What was the one TV program which was not a Super Bowl that broke into this top 10 list?

_____

_____

3. Which Super Bowl had the largest crowd in attendance? Where was it played? Who were the teams? What was the score? Who won? How many people were in the stands?

_____

_____

_____

4. What present AFC team played only one season as an NFC team? There is also a reverse of this question: What present NFC team played one season as an AFC team? What three AFC teams began in the National Football League and switched to the AFC at the time of the merger?

_____

_____

5. Some records are dubious records. For example, who holds the record for the most fumbles in a career in the NFL? Hint: He's still playing _(as of 1993)_ in the league, so the record may be getting larger.

_____

6. Which passer threw the most interceptions in his career? Hint: He also holds the record for most interceptions in a single season.

_____

Historical college trivia

1. The Rose Bowl was the first bowl game played at the end of the college season. Historically, any team could be invited to play. *(Now the champions of the Big 10 play the PAC 10 champs.)* So what four teams have won games in the Rose, Orange, Sugar, and Cotton bowls?

_____

_____

_____

2. What two college teams have played the most games against each other over the years?

_____

_____

3. What is the longest winning streak in college football history? Who was the team, how many games did they win, and over what seasons did the streak stretch?

_____

_____

4. What was the longest losing streak in college football history? Who was the team, how many games did they lose in a row, and over what seasons did the streak stretch?

_____

_____

_____

5. In 1936, which team won the first "national title" as voted on by the Associated Press writers' poll?

_____

_____

6. During World War II, there was a year when the Rose Bowl could not be played in California due to fears that the stadium might be bombed by the Japanese. The game was moved to the East Coast. What year was the game played, where was it played, and what teams played in it? Who won? By what score?

_____

_____

_____

_____

Modern college trivia

1. What quarterback attempted the most passes in one game? How many passes did he attempt? How many were completed? How many yards did he gain? For what team? Against who? Did the team win or lose?

_____

_____

_____

_____

_____

2. The mythical college championship is determined by voter polls. This system has been in place since 1936. How many years has it existed? How many times have their been co-champions? *(Consider only the major polls—the AP writers' poll and the UPI/CNN coaches' poll.)*

_____

_____

3. When was the first time that the number 1 ranked team played the number 2 ranked team?

_____

4. In the 1980s, one college team played the number 1 ranked team seven times and won every one of those games. Who was that team?

_____

5. Division I-AA football is played by colleges who are not as large as teams like Nebraska and UCLA. There is a play-off system to determine the champs of I-AA football. In 1991, '92, and '93 the same two teams played for the championship each year. Who were they? Who won each year?

_____

_____

6. What Ivy League school has won more football games than any other college? What major *(Division I-A)* college has won the most games?

_____

_____

Answer key

Answers vary in activities for which answers are not
provided below.

Miami Dolphin Records
1. $104
2. 288 points
3. 1030 receptions
4. 5,500 yards
5. 869 yards
6. 3152 yards

Lincoln's big win
1. 604 yards
2. 32 yards
3. 88 yards
4. 420 pushups
5. 76 players
6. 380 cups

Debbie's dogs
1. 1,500 hot dogs
2. 1,200 cups
3. 956 soft drinks
4. 1,848 nachos
5. 1,305 cups
6. 2,388 cups

Debbie's dollars and sense
1. $765.88
2. $449.28
3. $59.04
4. $348.70
5. $1,308.30
6. $2,931.20

Quarterback stats
1. 77 completions
2. 42%
3. 123 attempts
4. 46%
5. 105 attempts
6. 50 completions

Deee-fense
1. 15 fumbles
2. 30%
3. 30%
4. 140 tackles

Beasts of the East
1. 1,538.6 yards
2. 4,111 yards
3. 2,572.4 yards
4. 107.06 yards/game
5. 288.28 yards/game

Bobcats victory
1. 177 yards
2. 11.38 yards/cat
3. 8.6 yards/rush
4. 40.3 yards/punt
5. 89.4 yards

Why is it called football?
1. 434 points
2. 87 points
3. 21 field goals
4. 17 points
5. 155 PATs

They get a kick out of this
1. 30 field goals
2. 98.13%
3. 27 attempts
4. 82.20%
5. 37.5%

AFC rushing leaders
1. 520 yards
2. 3,177 yards
2a. 702 attempts
3. 17 yards

4. 167 attempts
5. 54 points
5a. 72 points
6. 11,896 yards

NFC rushing leaders
1. 3,065 yards
2. 108 points
3. 167 attempts
4. 43 yards
5. 12,840 yards

Home field advantage
1. 78.75%
2. 56–23
3. 34.18%
3a. 65.82%
4. 80
5. 62.03%

More home cooking
1a. 75.9%
1b. 75.0%
1c. 73.4%
1d. 67.5%
1e. 60.8%
1f. 58.8%
2. 78.1%
2a. 4.7%

"Shoes" and "Poppa Bear"
1. 48 games
2. 502 games
3. 803 games
4. 7 wins

The "best of the best"

Halas			
	8.1	3.8	.0
Shula			
	10.6	5.0	.2
Landry			
	9.3	6.1	.2
Lambeau			
	6.9	4.1	.7
Noll			
	9.1	6.8	.0
2.	Shula	Noll	

Monsters of the Midway
1. 132 yards/game
2. 4400 yards
3. 49 yards
4. 36 points
5. 516 points
6. 324 games

Los Angeles Rams records
1. 1,449 yards
2. varies
3. 119 yards
3a. 1,904 yards
4. 5140 yards
5. 5376 yards

Cleveland Brown heros
1. 9.67 games
2. 13,506 yards
3. 7 yards
4. 4,414 yards
5. Brown 1,368 yards

Cincinnati Bengals history
1. 36 points
2. 115 games
3. 115 games
4. 17 games
5. varies
6. 65 games

Indianapolis Colts history
1. 2339.29 yards
2. 1962 yards
3. JU by 377.29 yards
4. 44.77 yards
5. 108.17 yards

Silver and black attack
1. 66 games
2. 303 points
3. 943 PATs
4. 3,536 yards
5. 1,431 yards

Halftime munchies
1. $8.00
2. $10.00

3. 51 points
4. $21.00
5. $1.50

All-purpose yards leaders
1. 231 yards
2. 237 yards
3. 312 yards

College quarterback ratings
1. 74.51 rating

Forward and backward
1. 353 total yards
2. 434 net yards
3. 382 net yards
4. 302 total yards
5. 631 net yards
6. -59 yards

Football fashions
1. $1,225.00
   $980.00
   $630.00
   $280.00
   $210.00
   $1,575.00
   $1,620.00
   $720.00
   $2,340.00
   $175.00
   $184.00
2. $1,050.00
3. $140.00
4. $138.00
5. $558.00

New York Jet records
1. 558 PATs
2. 174 points
3. 444 points
4. 252 points
5. 8 field goals

Buffalo Bill records
1. 6,421 people
2. 3,822 yards
2a. 1,819 yards

3. 271 PATs
4. 99 points
5. 7.18 = 8 years

Detroit Lion records
1. 58.4 yards
2. 6.32 yards
3. 1,477.4 yards
4. 21 points
5. 101,598 people

Dallas Cowboy Super Bowls
1. 23 years
2. 194 points
3. 115 points
4. 27.71 points
4a. 16.43 points
5. $129,000
6. $1,728,000

Kansas City Chiefs history
1. 82 minutes, 40 seconds
2. 77 minutes, 54 seconds
3. 6 TDs
4. 35 points

Pre-game pep
1. $106.00
2. 53 banners
3. 8 1/6 yards
4. 12 strips
5. 5 5/12 yards

Crazy college capers
1. 25
2. 54 yards
3. 25 - 20 No PAT was attempted.

Wheeling and dealing
1. 6 points
2. 66 points
3. 108 points
4. 80.25 yards
5. 307.8 yards

Answer key

Football cards

1. Jeri must begin with seven cards and Barbara must begin with five cards. If this is the case, then when Jeri tries to give one to Babara, they would both have six cards. But when Barbara refuses that and then gives one card to Jeri, Jeri then has eight cards and Barbara is reduced to four. Thus, Jeri would have twice as many as Barbara.

2. The key to this problem is the phrase "each club member paid the same amount." That means something must divide into $2.89 evenly. When we test the possible factors 289, we find that the number can be divided evenly in only one way: 17 x 17. Therefore, 17 club members each paid 17 cents in dues. Again, there is only one way to use 5 coins to make 17 cents: 3 nicels and 2 pennies. Therefore, 17 club members paid 3 nickels each, so the club received 51 nickels.

How big Is the team?

1. The correct answer is 26 players. This solution is shown in the Venn Diagram.

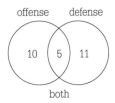

A common mistake is to add 15 and 16 to get a "solution" of 31. This method does not take into account that five players play on both squads. These players are counted twice in the mistaken procedure. A correct procedure is to note that five players play on both squads and since the number of offensive players is 15, then 10 (15-5) players are offensive specialists. By similar logic, 11 (16-5) players are defensive specialists. Adding the number of offense specialists, the number of defensive specialists, and the number of two-way players gives the correct answer of 26 total players.

A second method of calculating the correct answer is to add the number of offensive players (15) to the number of defensive players (16) and then subtract the number of players (5) that play on both squads. This gives the equation 15 +1 6 - 5 = 26, which is the correct answer.

2. There are 76 players on the Cougar football team. This solution is shown in the Venn Diagram.

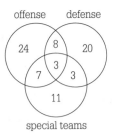

There are three players that play on all three squads. This number must be used to determine each of the other numbers. Since there are 11 players who play offense and defense, but three play on all the squads, eight players play offense and defense only. By similar reasoning, seven players play defense and special teams only and three players play on offense and special teams only. Since there are 42 total defensive players, and 18 (8+3+7) also participate on other squads, 24 players must play defense only. Similar reasoning results in 20 offensive specialists and 11 special teams only players. The results of this reasoning are shown in the Venn diagram above. (Students should be encouraged to draw diagrams such as one method of solving problems.) Then adding each of these numbers gives the total of 76 players on the Cougar football team.

Rapid runners

1. This problem requires several steps to solve it. One possible solution is:

> a. Find the average gain that Cesar has for each game.
> 387/3 = 129 yards per game.

> b. Then, multiple that average by 8 to see what the total projected yards would be for the season, if that pace is continued.
> 129 * 8 = 1032 yards per season.

The answer, then, is that is Cesar holds this average for the remaining five games, he will gain 1,032 yards during the season. That would be an excellent season for an eight game season.

2. One of the numbers needed to answer this problem is not given; we must find it. How many yards did Jorge improve between the two years? To find this, we subtract:

1093 - 758 = 335 more yards rushing in his senior year.

This is the improvement. Therefore, we must work the percentage problem with this number compared to the original, or the junior year, yardage. The ratio is set up as:

335 x   758 100

After cross multiplying, we obtain 33,500/758, which yields a percentage of 44.20%. This is Jorge's percentage improvement.

Winner's edge
1. This is an exercise in following the directions in the best order to get a solution. The limits—b and e—reduce the possible answers quickest. The answer must be between 82 and 98. Using "a", it must be an odd number, 83 to 97. Using "d", it must be an odd number that is a multiple of three; this reduces our possible answers to 87 and 93. When we examine "c", we find that only 93 gives an even number when you sum the digits. Therefore, the answer is 93.

2. Nineteen points could be scored in a variety of ways, shown as follows: (For ease of showing all answers, the words are omitted from the answer. Student might be asked to write how the score is made using football terms.)

7+7+3+2 = 19
6+3+3+3+2+2 = 19
7+6+3+3 = 19
3+3+3+3+3+2+2 = 19
7+3+3+3+3 = 193+3+3+2+2+2+2+2= 19
6+6+3+2+2 = 19
3+2+2+2+2+2+2+2+2 = 19
7+6+6 = 19

14 points could be scored as follows:
7+7   = 14   6+6+2   = 14
7+3+2+2 = 14   3+3+2+2+2+2= 14

Discussion: Which are most possible?

19 = Three touchdowns, but only one extra point. After missing the second, they went for two on the third and didn't make it.

19 = Two touchdowns, two two-point conversions, and a field goal.

14 = Two touchdowns and two PATs. By far the easiest.

Defensive delights
1. One way to solve this problem would be to make an ordered table. The table would have to show that there were twice as many assisted tackles as solo tackles. Therefore, the table would be:

Solo tackles	Assisted tackles	Points
1	2	4
2	4	8
3	6	12
4	8	16

Since we have now reached 16 points with twice as many assisted tackles, we know we have the answer and the table is done.

2. Tank must wear a number between 60 and 79. That is given by the hint. One assumption that can be made is that Tank's number must be in the 70s, because the first digit is a prime number. 6 is not prime; 7 is.

Then, since the first digit is a prime number, and both digits add to be that prime number, only 70, 74, and 76 add up to be prime numbers. But only 70 gives a 7 for an answer. Therefore, Tank wears the number 70.

Scoring schemes I
1. This problem has an algebraic solution. The equation should be made with x equaling the number of points scored on place kicks and 4x being the number of points scored on field goals. Therefore,

$x + 4x = 135$
$5x = 135$
$x = 27$
$4x = 108$

So, Karl the Kicker scored 27 points on PATs and 108 points on field goals. This means he made 27 PATs and 108/3 field goals, or 36 field goals.

Children in grades 4–8 do not know algebra; they will have to invent the solution. They may use several different strategies, as "guess and check" or making a systematic list to get the solution.

2. One way to solve this is to make a systematic list. Since the Hokies scored seven times, they will have between 7 TDs/0 field goals and 0 TDs/7 field goals. Therefore:

TDs	FGoals	Total points
7	0	49
6	1	45
5	2	41
4	3	37
3	4	33 - The score.
2	5	29
1	6	25
0	7	21

Therefore: The Hokies scored 3 touchdowns and 4 field goals.

Helpful heroes I
1. Since Toady Tom is so fussy, Bill will have to do the following:

1. Fill up the three-cup container. Pour that water into the five-cup container.

2. Then fill up the three cups again, and pour as much water into the five-cup container as you can. That will be two cups, leaving one cup in the three-cup container.

3. Empty the five-cup container. The pour in the one cup of water left in the three-cup container.

4. Then fill up the three-cup container again and pour into the five-cup container.
   The five-cup container will now hold the one cup + three cups, which equals four cups of water. Toady Tom can now have his drink.

2. The simplest way to answer this question is to make a list of the number of pushups the Tiger does after each TD. The problem is simplified by the fact that Clemson only scored touchdowns. The problem solver does not have to consider other scoring plays. First, 84 divided by 7 = 12 TDs.

After Clemson's	1st TD:	7 pushups
	2nd TD:	14 pushups
	3rd TD:	21 pushups
	4th TD:	29 pushups
	5th TD:	35 pushups
	6th TD:	42 pushups
	7th TD:	49 pushups
	8th TD:	56 pushups
	9th TD:	63 pushups
	10th TD:	70 pushups
	11th TD:	77 pushups
	12th TD:	84 pushups

Then total all the pushups: 546 pushups in all.

Mathematician Karl Frederick Gauss developed a formula for finding the sum of the first n counting numbers; that formula can be modified to obtain the answer to this problem. Gauss's formula is:
$$S = n * (n+1)$$ where n is the number of numbers being added.

In this problem, n = 12 because Clemson scored 12 touchdowns and we are finding the sum of the first 12 counting numbers. This formula gives an answer 78. But we are working with touchdowns, we must multiply this answer by 7. This provides us with 78 * 7 = 546. This logic is a simplified version of what the mathematician would actually do; but it is a good example of how a student may modify a formula to solve a problem.

Darrell's deeds
1. One solution uses a variation of the Distance = Rate x Time problem, with an interesting twist. It can best be solved by using a ratio. The ratio would be set up to say, "If Darrell can run 40 yards in 4.2

seconds, then how many yards could he run in 3,600 seconds? (3,600 seconds = one hour.) So:

40 yards:	x yards
4.2 seconds	3600 seconds

After cross multiplying and dividing, we find that Darrell could run 34,285 yards in an hour. This give us the "yards per hour" rate. So, we divide by 1,760 yards in a mile to find the "miles per hour" rate.

It comes out to be 19.48 miles per hour.

2. This problem can be solved by making a ratio, but some thought has to go into the ratio. The usual units for a mile are not be used. The problem states that Darrell is being timed in the 40-yard dash. So, the ratio has to be:

4.2 seconds:	x seconds
40 yards	1760 YARDS in a mile

The answer, after cross multiplying, would be 184.8 seconds. That translates into 3 minutes and 4.8 seconds.

Scoring schemes II

1. Since, in this problem, Seattle scored ten points less than half as many as New England, we have to work backwards. New England scored 186 points. Half of that figure is 93 points. Ten less is 83 points. Therefore, Seattle would have scored 83 points in this situation.

Actually, Seattle scored 140 points. The next lowest team in the NFL was New England, they scored 205 points. Seattle did have a "bad year." In fact, Steve Christie, the kicker for Buffalo, score 115 by himself. He almost outscored Seattle singlehandedly.

2. The algebraic formula and computation for this problem would be:

1/2x + 1/4x + 1/6x + 3 = x. Find a common denominator:

6/12x + 3/12x+ 2/12x + 3 = x
11/12 x + 3 = x
3 = x - 11/12x
3 = 1/12 x
36 = x

Sam has played in 36 games. He has scored three TDs in 18 games, 2 TDs in 9 games, and one TD in six games. He did not score in 3 games. 18 + 9 + 6 + 3 = 36. He scored, then, 18(3) + 9(2) + 6(1) equals 78 TDs, which equals 468 points in the 36 games.

Helpful heroes II

1. One way to find average speed is divide the total distance by the total time. The distance for the first leg of the trip is not given. So, we must find it:

20 miles per hour times 2/3 of an hour (40 minutes) equals a distance of 13.33 miles.

The second part of the trip was given as 100 miles; therefore, the entire trip was 113.33 miles.

But, we also need to find the total time. The first leg is given at 40 minutes. We must obtain the second.

100 miles/70 miles per hour = 1.43 hours.

The total time was 1.43 hours + .67 hours (40 minutes) = 2.10 hours.

The average rate, then, is found by dividing 113.33 miles by 2.10 hours. This divides to be 53.97 miles per hour.

If the trip was planned at 2 hours, and it took 2.10 hours, how many minutes were they early or late? Obviously, they were late by .10 hours; this translates to 6 minutes, since 60 x .10 = 6. It is a common mistake for students to translate ".10 hours" to 10 minutes. Watch for it.

2. This problem requires simultaneous equations, a topic which is not taught until first or second year algebra. That procedure is not available to students in grades 4 to 8. They must use another procedure. Making a systematic list will get the answer. The problem with this solution is there are 31 different whole-number combinations to examine, but there is no guarantee the answer will not include decimals. That possibility increases the list to a potentially infinite series of combinations.

Using a "guess and check" strategy, along with some logical thinking, can reduce the number of combinations to be checked. Consider:

First: Let's "guess" they made equal amounts. What would happen if Fred and Carrie both made 15 pounds of caramel corn?

> Carrie's 15 pounds is 70% popcorn. This is 10.5 pounds of popcorn.
> Fred's 15 pounds is 60% popcorn. This is nine pounds of popcorn.
> Together, they would have used 19.5 pounds of popcorn.

This is **MORE** than the 19 pounds of popcorn available. Logic: The 19.5 pounds of popcorn is too much. Since Carrie uses more popcorn in her mix, our next guess should reduce the Carrie's amount.

Second: Let's "guess" that Carrie made 12 pounds and Fred 18 pounds.

> Carrie's 12 pounds is 70% popcorn. This is 8.4 pounds of popcorn.
> Fred's 18 pounds is 60% popcorn. This is 10.8 pounds of popcorn.
> Together, they would have used 19.2 pounds of popcorn.

This are still more than the 19 pounds of popcorn available. Logic: Answer still too large. Reduce Carrie still more.

Third: Let's "guess" that Carrie makes 9 pounds and Fred 21 pounds. Using the same procedure, we see that this guess uses only 18.9 pounds of popcorn. We are now under the 19 pounds. We've gone too far. and Fred 20 pounds. Using the same procedure, we see that this is the correct answer.

Fourth: Let's guess that Carrie makes 10 pounds

Mini-projects and long-term projects
Answers will vary.

Collecting trivia information
Historical NFL trivia
1. Chicago Bears. Began as the Decatur Staleys in 1920, moved to Chicago in 1921, and played as the Chicago Staleys. Became the Chicago Bears in 1922. George Halas bought the team in 1921.

Phoenix Cardinals. Started as the Chicago Cardinals. Played in Chicago from 1920 to 1959. Moved to St. Louis and played there from 1960 to 1987. They moved to Phoenix in 1988 and have played there ever since.

2. The Green Bay Packers began play in the NFL in 1921. They have not moved, nor have they changed their name since that time.

3a. The Tonawanda Kardex. They played 1 game in the 1921 season and lost. They concluded their NFL career with a record of 0 wins and 1 loss.

3b. The Muncie Flyers. They played and lost 1 game in the 1920 season. They played and lost 2 games in the 1921 season. Their combined NFL record, therefore, is 0 wins and 3 losses.

3c. The Frankford Yellow Jackets. In the 1925 season, they played 20 regular season games. Their record was 13 wins and 7 losses.

3d. The first meeting in 1920 selected the name "The American Professional Football Conference." At the second organizational meeting, the name was changed to "The American Professional Football Association." The first games in 1920 were played under the APFA banner.

3e. The first game between two APFA teams was played on October 3, 1920. The Dayton Triangles hosted the Columbus Panhandles. Dayton won, 14 to 0. The first touchdown was scored by Lou Partlow of Dayton. (Later that same day, the Rock Island Independents defeated the Muncie Flyers 45-0. This game ended Muncie's season that year.)

4. Jim Thorpe played for the Canton Bulldogs. Canton is now the home of the Professional Football Hall of Fame.

Modern NFL trivia

1. Y. A. Tittle and George Blanda each threw 36 TD passes in a season. Thus, they were responsible for 216 points, while Marino was responsible for 288 points. (This figures 6 points for the TD, as the kicker gets the extra point.)

2. The last episode of M*A*S*H was a two-hour movie shown on February 28, 1983. This movie ranked number 4 on the all-time list. All the other top 10 shows were Super Bowls. Officially, Super Bowls 27, 20, 21, 26, 19, 22, 25, 23, and 16—in that order.

3. Super Bowl 14, played in the Rose Bowl in Pasadena, California. There were 103,985 people in the stands. The Pittsburgh Steelers defeated the Los Angeles Rams by a score of 31-19.

4. Seattle Seahawks in 1976. Similarly, the Tampa Bay Bucs played that same year in the AFC. Both expansion teams played their first season in the opposite league from their current location. When the AFC was formed in 1970, the Cleveland Browns, the Pittsburgh Steelers, and the Baltimore (now Indianapolis) Colts moved from the NFL into the AFC to make the two conferences the same size.

5. Dave Kreig of the Seattle Seahawks and Kansas City Chiefs. As of the beginning of the 1993 season, he had fumbled 118 times.

6. George Blanda. His career spanned 26 seasons. He threw 277 interceptions over this time. He threw 42 interceptions in the 1962 season of the old AFL. This is accepted as an NFL record.

Historical college trivia

1. Alabama, Georgia, Georgia Tech, and Notre Dame. All of these teams played in the Rose Bowl before 1947, when the present Big 10 and PAC 10 playoff started in the Rose Bowl.

2. Lafayette and Lehigh. They have played each other 134 times as of the end of the 1993 football season. No other rivalry is close to this number.

3. Oklahoma won 47 games in a row over seasons, spanning 1953-1957.

4. The Columbia Lions lost 44 games in a row over seasons spanning 1983-1988.

5. The Minnesota Gophers.

6. In 1942, Oregon State played Duke for the Rose Bowl game, but the game was held at Duke Stadium in Durham, North Carolina. Oregon State won the game, 20 to 16.

Modern college trivia

1. Paul Gray, of Hanover College in Indiana, threw 92 passes in one game. He completed 41 of them for 630 yards of total offense and 7 TDs, but his team still lost to Georgetown (KY) College, 55 to 46. This was a NAIA Division II game. He was quoted as saying "I'm numb." after the game.

2. Since 1936, the following 10 seasons had co-champions:

1947	Notre Dame and Michigan
1954	Ohio State and UCLA
1957	Auburn and Ohio State
1965	Alabama and Michigan State
1970	Nebraska and Texas
1973	Notre Dame and Alabama
1974	Oklahoma and Southern Cal
1978	Alabama and Southern Cal
1990	Colorado and Georgia Tech
1991	Miami and Washington

3. On October 9, 1943, number 2 Michigan beat number 1 Notre Dame by a score of 35-12.

4. The Miami Hurricanes.

5. The teams were the Marshall "Thundering Herd" and the "Youngstown Penguins." Youngstown won in 1991 and 1993; Marshall won in 1992. The scores were:

1991	Youngstown	25	Marshall	17
1992	Marshall	31	Youngstown	28
1993	Youngstown	17	Marshall	5

6. Yale has won 760 games as of 1990. Michigan has won 712 games in 1-A competition.